THE POET PROPHETS OF THE
OLD TESTAMENT

The Rt Revd Robert Lowth DD FRS
(1710-1787)
Bishop of London and
Oxford Professor of Poetry

Portrait by Robert Edge Pine (1730-1788)
© Courtesy of the Warden & Scholars of New College Oxford

The Poet Prophets
of the Old Testament

Beauchief Abbey Lectures 2017

J. W. Rogerson

BEAUCHIEF
ABBEY·PRESS

Published by Beauchief Abbey Press, February 2018
www.beauchiefabbeypress.org.uk

ISBN 978-0-9935499-6-0

A CIP catalogue record for this title is available from the British
Library.

Cover design by Michael Lindley, Truth Studio, Studio 15, Sum
Studios, 1 Hartley Street, Sheffield S2 3AQ. www.truthstudio.co.uk

Printed by www.lulu.com

Introduction

At the end of May 2016, I preached a sermon at Llansantffraed Church, Powys as part of the Coleridge in Wales Festival. This project was an eighty-day journey around Wales, following routes that had been taken by the poet, philosopher and theologian Samuel Taylor Coleridge in 1794 and 1802. It was designed and carried out by Richard Parry, who not only followed Coleridge's routes, but spoke to people that he met about Coleridge, British culture and Christianity, and also organised activities illustrative of the project at various points in the journey. Further information can be found on the website at www.coleridgeinwales.org.

The basic inspiration for the project came from Richard's membership of the congregation of Beauchief Abbey in Sheffield, and the Abbey's commitment to the Broad Church theology to which Coleridge made a fundamental contribution himself and through his followers, including F. D. Maurice and Charles Kingsley.

My sermon, which appears in this book as the Prologue, dealt with the subject of prophecy as poetry, a theme appropriate to the celebration of Coleridge and to the fact that the poet Henry

Vaughan is buried in the churchyard at Llansantffraed. The aim of the Lent Lectures at Beauchief Abbey in 2017 was to develop further the themes explored in that sermon.

I do not pretend that a book reprinting five lectures will make a substantial or original contribution to the understanding of Old Testament prophecy; but I have tried to say some original things and to concentrate on aspects of Old Testament prophecy that are often overlooked. I would also like to think that the book might be a useful introduction to Old Testament prophecy for beginners.

Once again, I am grateful to the congregation of Beauchief Abbey for the opportunity to give the lectures and to Richard Parry for his bold and imaginative ways of reaching out beyond the walls of the Abbey to those outside.

J. W. Rogerson
Sheffield, October 2017

CONTENTS

'Where there is no vision ...'

The Word of the LORD was rare in those days; there was no frequent vision.[1]

With those words, the writer of the First Book of Samuel introduced the story of the call of Samuel to be a prophet. He went on to relate how Samuel with his groups of prophets enabled the Israelites to overcome, first, the disasters of defeat and subjugation by the Philistines and, second, how under the leadership of Saul and then of David, the Israelites were able to set up a small kingdom, with the capital in Jerusalem. This small nation became the people of God, and from the people of God there emerged what we call the 'Old Testament prophets'. It is worth reminding ourselves that the Old Testament prophets are the people to whom the world owes the gift of what we call 'ethical monotheism' – the belief in one Creator God, a God of righteousness, justice, mercy and compassion. It was not the great and advanced civilisations of the Ancient World that gave to the world that precious gift. It

---

[1] 1 Samuel 3.1 Revised Standard Version. The Hebrew word translated 'frequent' literally means 'spread [abroad]'.

was not Assyria, or Babylon, or Egypt, or Rome, or even Greece, but a small group of prophets from the tiny and culturally insignificant nation of the Israelites that gave to the world this precious gift of ethical monotheism.

I have started speaking about the Old Testament prophets, because the Old Testament prophets were poets. I hope you may have noticed in our readings today that something came over in them of the nature of Old Testament poetry. In that great chapter from Isaiah, chapter 40, we have these marvellously balanced parallel phrases:

> Hast thou not known? hast thou not heard, that the everlasting God, the LORD Creator of the ends of the earth, fainteth not, neither is weary? There is no searching of his understanding. He giveth power to the faint; and to those that have no might he increaseth strength. Even the youths shall faint and be weary, and the young men shall fail: But they that wait upon the LORD shall renew their strength; they shall mount up with wings as eagles; they shall run, and not be weary; they shall walk and not be faint. (Isaiah 40.28-31)

You may have noticed something of the same thing in the reading from the Sermon on the Mount, for some of the teaching of Jesus is similarly framed in terms of Hebrew poetic parallelism:

> Therefore I say unto you, Take no thought for your life, what ye shall eat, or what ye shall drink; nor yet for your body, what ye shall put on. Is not the life more than meat, and the body more than raiment? (Matthew 6.25)

Why did the Old Testament prophets use poetic diction? They were, of course, speaking to their own people in their own language. But this was not the language of the marketplace, the language of the family, or the language of gossip at the street corners. It was the language of God addressing his people, and because it was poetic language, God's message had a dignity, a resonance, a solemnity which ordinary language would not have conveyed. But there is more to it than that. The prophets were also poets, in that they possessed what we might call 'the poetic imagination'. We tend to think of prophets as people who foretold the future, but the prophets, like the greatest of poets, were not so much people who foresaw the future, but people who spoke about the present, people who saw the present in ways that no-one else could see it, people who spoke about the present in ways that no-one else could speak about it. Their language had a depth and surplus of meaning so that what they said resonated far beyond their own times and spoke to many generations to come. In viewing the present as they did, they spoke of what we might call an 'eternal now' that was to be found in the present, and indeed is to be found in all presents – past and present and future. If their words seemed to be prophetic and forecasting the future, it was rather because they were speaking about an eternal now, which, because it was present also in the present of later generations, seemed to speak and resonate with them. This is why we today honour the poets: Shakespeare, four hundred years after his death, Coleridge, Henry Vaughan, George Herbert. They speak to our present, because in speaking of their own present, they articulated something of the eternal now.

I am going to read some words to you that will be familiar from the second part of Handel's *Messiah*, but I am not going to read them in the version that Handel used – the Authorized, or King James, Bible – but I am going to read them in the Geneva Version of 1560. I am going to do this because the great translators of the Geneva Bible were the first scholars to put into English the very difficult Hebrew of the poetic parts of the Old Testament – and the Geneva Bible was the Bible of Shakespeare. It was the Bible also often referred to by Henry Vaughan, honoured and buried here in Llansantffraed. In fact, the Geneva Bible translators did such a good job that all the Authorized Version translators had to do was to alter the odd word here and there. People have spoken about the 'Hebraising' of the English Language, because of the way in which the translation into English of these cadences and resonances of Hebrew came into the English Language, through Shakespeare, particularly, and also then later through the Authorized Version.

As I read to you these words from Isaiah 53 in the Geneva Version, you will be forgiven for thinking that I am actually reading the Authorized Version:

> He is despised and rejected of men: he is a man of sorrows and hath experience of infirmities: we hid as it were our faces from him: he was despised, and we esteemed him not. Surely he hath borne our infirmities and carried our sorrows: yet we did judge him as plagued, and smitten of God, and humbled. But he was wounded for our transgressions, he was broken for our iniquities: the chastisement of our peace was upon him, and with his stripes we are healed. All we like sheep have gone astray: we have turned every one to his own way, and the Lord hath laid upon him the iniquity of us all. (Isaiah 53.3-6)

In these words, the prophet is speaking about his own time. He is speaking about someone – we don't know who it was – who had suffered, who had suffered willingly on behalf of others, although those others at the time did not appreciate what he was doing. And in the words that we have heard, the prophet speaks of that suffering servant and says that his sufferings did in fact bring healing and reconciliation to some of his contemporaries, as now they realise. In speaking in this way about his present, the prophet/poet spoke of an eternal now, of the way in which suffering, voluntarily offered up and undertaken on behalf of others, can bring healing and reconciliation. Of course it is no accident that these words have been seen to be supremely applicable to the life, and ministry, and death of Jesus, and have been seen as prophecies of his saving work: because they are that – but also because they are speaking about an eternal now in the prophet's present.

What this boils down to is that we desperately need prophets, and we desperately need poets. We need to hear them speaking about the eternal now in our own present; because if we do not hear them, then we shall conceive humankind in narrow, materialistic, monetary ways. We shall forget that humans are spiritual beings with an eternal destiny. In that case, alas! it will be true of the present generation what the writer of the First Book of Samuel said about the generation of Samuel's call:

> The Word of the LORD was rare in those days; there was
> no vision [by which is meant 'vision of prophecy'].
> (1 Samuel 3.1)

There is another text, which is often quoted and which was a favourite of Coleridge, from the Book of Proverbs:

> Where there is no vision [vision of prophecy], the people
> perish. (Proverbs 29.18)

And so we need the Old Testament prophets, and we need poets, which is why the Coleridge in Wales Festival is so important. We need poets and poetry, not only in our everyday lives; we need them in our worship, in our theology, in our services, because without poetry these things will become impoverished.

I want to end by reading two pieces which, in their different ways, are poetry. The first is a prayer that I often use at funerals, and people often ask me where these words come from, because they are so beautifully poetic and indeed draw to some extent upon that marvellous collection of poems in the Old Testament that we call the Song of Songs, or the Song of Solomon. The words are by Cardinal John Henry Newman:

> O Lord,
> Support us all the day long of this troublous life,
> until the shades lengthen and the evening comes,
> and the busy world is hushed,
> the fever of life is over, and our work is done.
> Then, Lord, in thy mercy,
> grant us a safe lodging, a holy rest,
> and peace at the last.

The other piece is a poem, by the priest-poet Sidney Royse Lysaght (1856-1941). It is entitled, 'The Penalty of Love', and you can read it, as you can all poems, in several ways. You can think of it as speaking of poetry and how we are impoverished without it, or you can read it in terms of love in its purest, noblest, strongest sense, or you can read it in terms of the love of God incarnate and brought to us in Jesus Christ.

> If love should count you worthy, and should deign
> One day to seek your door and be your guest,
> Pause! ere you draw the bolt and bid him rest,
> If in your old content you would remain.
> For not alone he enters: in his train
> Are angels of the mists, the lonely quest,
> Dreams of the unfulfilled and unpossessed.
> And sorrow, and life's immemorial pain.
> He wakes desires you never may forget,

He shows you stars you never saw before,
He makes you share with him for evermore,
The burden of the world's divine regret
How wise were you to open not!--and yet,
How poor if you should turn him from the door.

**Authorized Version
Isaiah 40.4-5**

Every valley shall be exalted, and every
mountain and hill shall be made low:
and the crooked shall be made straight, and
the rough places plain:

And the glory of the LORD shall be revealed,
and all flesh shall see it together: for the
mouth of the LORD hath spoken it.

**Revised Standard Version
Isaiah 40.4-5**

Every valley shall be lifted up,
  and every mountain and hill be made low;
the uneven ground shall become level,
  and the rough places a plain.

And the glory of the LORD shall be revealed,
  and all flesh shall see it together,
    for the mouth of the LORD has spoken.

Comparison of layout between the Authorized Version
and the Revised Standard Version *(see facing page)*

LECTURE 1

The Rediscovery of Biblical Hebrew Poetry in the Eighteenth Century

'Robert Lowth changed the way we read the Bible.' So wrote James L Kugel towards the end of his book, *The Idea of Biblical Poetry*.[2] He could have added that Robert Lowth changed the way the Bible is printed. If you compare the way in which Isaiah chapter 40 is laid out in the Authorized Version and the Revised Standard Version you will notice a difference *(see facing page)*.

The Authorized Version prints each verse separately. The Revised Standard Version breaks each verse into shorter units in an attempt to indicate the parallelisms that each contains. This is the legacy of Robert Lowth. Who was he, how did he change our way of printing and reading the Bible, and how should we evaluate his legacy?

---

[2] J. L. Kugel, *The Idea of Biblical Poetry. Parallelism and its History*, New Haven and London: Yale University Press, 1981, p. 286.

Lowth was born in the cathedral close in Winchester on 8th December 1710, his father being a Prebendary, or canon, of Winchester. He was educated at the local prestigious public school of Winchester and proceeded to Winchester's twin foundation in Oxford, New College. In 1735 he became Vicar of Overton in Hampshire and in 1741 he was elected to the professorship of poetry in the University of Oxford, in which position he delivered 35 lectures in Latin over the course of a number of years, which were published in Latin in 1753 under the title *On the Sacred Poetry of the Hebrews*.[3] In 1778 Lowth published a new translation of the Book of Isaiah, with a preliminary dissertation of over 90 pages, in which he repeated and refined the arguments of his earlier lectures, applying them essentially to the Book of Isaiah.[4] In 1750 Lowth became Archdeacon of Westminster, in 1755 a Prebend of Durham, in 1766 Bishop of Oxford, and in 1778 Bishop of London, where he died on 3rd November 1787, aged 76.

Why did Lowth need to change the way we read the Bible? This can be illustrated by something familiar, the account in Matthew's Gospel of the triumphal entry of Jesus into Jerusalem on Palm Sunday (21.1-5). In the Gospels of Mark (11.1-2) and Luke (19.28-30) Jesus sends disciples to Bethphage and Bethany to find a colt on which he will ride into Jerusalem. They do so, and he rides on it. In John (12.14) it is Jesus himself who finds a young ass and rides upon it. Matthew is different. Disciples are sent to Bethphage to

---

[3] R. Lowth, *Memoirs of the Life and Worship of the late Right Reverend Robert Lowth*, London: W. Best, 1787.
For the lectures, reference is made to R. Lowth, *De sacra poesie Hebraeorum. Praelectiones Academicae*, Oxford: Clarendon Press 1810. 2 vols. with annotations by J. D. Michaelis, English translation by G. Gregory, *Lectures on the Sacred Poetry of the Hebrews*, 2 vols, London: J. Johnson, 1787, this edition includes the notes by Michaelis and others.
[4] R. Lowth, *Isaiah. A New Translation with a Preliminary Dissertation and Notes*, Glasgow: Longman and others, 1822.

procure *two* animals - an ass and a colt. The disciples put garments on the two animals and Jesus sits upon them; whether 'them' means the garments or the two animals is not clear. Why does Matthew have two animals? It is because he takes literally the prophecy in Zechariah 9.9:

> Tell ye the daughter of Sion, Behold, thy king cometh unto thee, meek, and sitting upon an ass, and a colt, the foal of an ass. (Zechariah 9.9, quoted in Matthew 21.5)

The significant word is the 'and' which comes before the words 'a colt'. Matthew takes it to convey additional information; to add something to what is said immediately beforehand. The Hebrew does indeed also have the word 'and', but it does not mean to provide additional information. In the Hebrew there is parallelism: the same thing is said in two ways. The ass and the colt the foal of an ass are not two distinct animals, but one animal described in two different ways. Lowth himself did not use this particular example from Matthew. I have done so in order to make the matter as clear and simple as possible; but Lowth used other examples from the Old Testament to argue that Hebrew poetry, whatever else it was, was characterised by parallelism, in which the same thing was described in two different ways.

Later on in this lecture it will be necessary to evaluate Lowth's arguments which, in spite of a certain amount of criticism and refinement, have generally stood the test of time.[5] For the moment, it has to be asked why it was not until the first part of the eighteenth century that someone rediscovered this

---

[5] See G. B. Gray, *The Forms of Hebrew Poetry considered with Special Reference to the Criticism and Interpretation of the Old Testament*, London: Hodder and Stoughton, 1915; W. G. E. Watson, 'The Study of Hebrew Poetry: Past – Present – Future in J. Jarick (ed.), *Sacred Conjectures. The Context and Legacy of Robert Lowth and Jean Astruc*, New York: T. & T. Clark, 2007, pp. 124-54.

characteristic feature of Hebrew poetry. How did it come about that the nature of Hebrew poetry was forgotten for more than 1500 years until it was rediscovered in the eighteenth century? The most exhaustive study of this matter is that by James L. Kugel in the book mentioned at the beginning of the lecture. He lists a number of factors that contributed to what can best be called the background to Lowth's work, a background that makes clear the importance of that work.

First, there is the fact that the Jewish interpreters of the Bible who worked in the early centuries of the Common Era believed that anything and everything in the Bible was significant, however obscure it might appear. The fact that the Bible often described the same thing in two different ways meant, for these interpreters, as with the example of Matthew's account of the triumphal entry, that two things, not one were being described. A common practice was for one statement to be referred to the present world, and for the other to be referred to the world to come. Thus a text such as Psalm 146.1

> While I live will I praise the Lord,
> Yea, as long as I have any being, I will sing praises unto
> my God

would be read as follows: 'while I live' refers to the present world, and 'as long as I have any being' refers to the world to come.[6]

The second factor was the system of punctuation of the Hebrew Bible that was devised by the scholars of Tiberias, and that became standard in the manuscript tradition. It made a

---

[6] Kugel, p. 97.

distinction between books regarded by them as poetic – Job, Psalms and Proverbs – and the rest which were not, therefore, regarded as poetic.[7] Third, with the spread of Greek culture among Jews from the fourth century BC, Greek poetry became sufficiently familiar to some Jewish scholars to become the norm by which poetry was to be distinguished from prose. Hebrew texts did not conform to the Greek norms and were therefore not regarded as poetry. Fourth, when a tradition of Hebrew poetry did emerge in the Middle Ages, from roughly the tenth century onwards, it was based upon Arabic models in which, among other things, every line of verse ended with the same rhyme. Rhyme is not an obvious feature of biblical Hebrew texts.[8]

Kugel's chapter entitled 'Biblical Poetry and the Church' covers a great deal of ground, and comments on the attempts of scholars such as Origen (c. 185/6-253/4) and Jerome (c. 347-419/20) who knew Hebrew, to argue that Hebrew poetry was characterised by metre, even though by their time the way in which Hebrew was pronounced in the biblical period had been forgotten.[9] Any attempt, therefore, to rediscover Hebrew poetic metre was bound to fail. However, the sum total of their efforts meant that in the Christian Church it was accepted that Hebrew poetry, principally in the Psalms and Job, was metrical. Ironically, Christian interpreters were not blind to the phenomenon of parallelism, but did not see it as an essential part of Hebrew poetry.

The picture of how things stood immediately before Lowth began his lectures in 1741 is hopefully beginning to take

---

[7] Kugel, pp. 109-116.
[8] Kugel, pp. 127-9.
[9] Kugel, p. 153, note 58, shows how Jerome failed to distinguish between `aleph* and `ayin* and between `ayin* and ḥeth*.

shape, but a little more detail is needed to complete it. We have to return to parallelism and metre.

Kugel shows how, in spite of the development of Jewish mediaeval Hebrew poetry based upon Arabic models, it was still possible for Jewish scholars to write hymns and prayers that copied the style of the biblical psalms, which used parallelism. They were writing in the style of biblical Hebrew poetry without realising what that implied! There were also two scholars who became aware of the phenomenon of parallelism, prior to Lowth. One was Azariah ben Moses dei Rossi (1511-78), who was indeed mentioned and quoted by Lowth.[10] He was a Jewish physician and scholar who lived and died in Mantua in Italy. In his great work *The Light of the Eyes* (1574) he discussed the nature of biblical poetry and reached the important conclusion that what mattered about it were not the words or syllables, but the ideas and the ways in which they were joined together. He made an important observation, which was quoted by Lowth:

> Do you not see that if you translate some of them [he meant the songs of the prophets] into another language they still keep and retain their measure [their ideas] if not wholly at least in part? which cannot be the case in those verses, the measures of which arise from a certain quantity and number of syllables.[11]

In other words, he was saying what will be apparent to English readers of translations of, say, Isaiah 40 in the Authorized Version, that whatever the metrical principles of the poem may have been, if any, the juxtaposition of the ideas is clear even in translation.

---

[10] Kugel, pp. 200-201.
[11] Lowth, *Isaiah*, p. lxiii. See also Lecture III, *De sacra poesie*, p. 42, English vol. 1, p. 72.

It is perhaps unfair to Lowth to mention at this point another scholar who was also working on the problem of the nature of biblical poetry and who in some ways anticipated Lowth – unfair because Lowth almost certainly did not know about his work. It was published in two volumes in Leipzig and Dresden in 1733 and 1742, and Lowth would surely have referred to it if he had known of it. I am referring to Johann Christian Schöttgen (1687-1751) who preferred a career as a schoolmaster to that of an academic, who was head of the distinguished grammar school in Dresden, and was also a prolific scholar.[12] In his *Horae Hebraicae et Talmudicae* (1733) he included a 15-page essay on what he called 'Exergasia' a Classical Greek word meaning 'completion', which in rhetoric was understood as the joining together of statements of the same significance.[13] It presupposed that a line of Hebrew poetry had two parts or clauses, in which the subject matter was joined in various ways. He set out ten rules, or examples, of how this joining together occurred, of which some anticipated Lowth's classifications. For example Rule One states that the content of the two clauses is so similar that the second adds nothing to the first. An example is found in Psalm 33.7:

> He gathers| as in a water skin| the waters of the sea,
> And places| as in a treasure house| the deeps.

This is close to what Lowth would call 'synonymous parallelism'. As I said a moment ago, it is perhaps unfair to Lowth to mention a contemporary scholar who almost beat him to the post, as it were, but it illustrates how, in the humanities just as much as in the sciences and technology, it can happen that scholars working in separate places can

---

[12] See G. Müller, 'Schöttgen, Johann Christoph' in *Allgemeine Deutsche Biographie*, 32 (1891), pp. 412-17.
[13] Kugel, p. 267.

independently reach similar conclusions or make similar discoveries that alter the course of knowledge.

Someone of whom Lowth was aware was Francis Hare (1671-1740), educated at Eton and King's College Cambridge, and who became Bishop of St Asaph (1727-1731) and of Chichester (1731-1740). In 1736, five years before Lowth began his Oxford lectures, Hare had published a work on the Hebrew psalms, in which he claimed to have discovered the poetic metre in which they were written.[14] Lowth disagreed so profoundly with Hare's theory that he wrote a refutation, which was appended to later editions of the Oxford lectures.[15] Lowth's basic objection to Hare's system was that it was inconsistent; that it required the same Hebrew word sometimes to consist of a long stressed syllable followed by a short one, at other times a short stressed syllable followed by a long one, and at other times to be two equally stressed syllables. This inconsistency was needed to make the facts fit a theory that was not based upon the facts.

It is time at last to focus fully on Lowth's work. As Kugel has written, 'By Lowth's time all the elements of the puzzle he was to deal with had been laid out. His task was primarily that of arrangement and synthesis – but this was no small matter'.[16] Lowth changed the way we read the Bible.

After two introductory lectures, Lowth turned directly to biblical poetry and the question of Hebrew metre. He believed that biblical poetry must have had a metre, but that it was not possible to recover it. 'He who attempts to restore the true and

---

[14] F. Hare, *Psalmorum liber, in versiculos metrice divisus*, 1736.
[15] Lowth, 'Metricae Harianae brevis confutatio' in *De sacra poesie*, pp. 463-70, English vol. 2, pp. 436-46.
[16] Kugel, p. 273.

genuine Hebrew versification erects an edifice without a foundation', he wrote.[17] How then was it possible to identify and describe biblical poetry if one of the fundamentals of poetry according to Greek and Latin models was beyond our reach? Lowth first made an observation that will not be lost on anyone who has studied biblical Hebrew. The learner 'who is a proficient in the historical books, when he comes to the poetical parts, will find himself almost a perfect stranger'.[18] Obviously, the fact, striking as it is, that when beginners in Hebrew get to poetic texts they find themselves confronted by words they do not know, joined together in ways they do not understand, does not constitute a satisfactory basis for defining Hebrew biblical poetry.

Lowth next set out from the fact that in the Psalms and elsewhere there exists a number of alphabetical or acrostic compositions, in which each line begins with a successive letter of the Hebrew alphabet. This provides a way of determining what a line of poetry consists of, because each line is complete before it begins with the next letter of the Hebrew alphabet. Thus delineated, it was apparent that each line consisted of two parts, in which the content of the second part connected in some way with the content of the first part. This would later be described as parallelism; but it was not until the eighteenth lecture that Lowth dealt with this, and in that lecture he defended the view that the bulk of the language of the prophetic books of the Old Testament was poetry, and he did so in a way that was conditioned by the limitations of the biblical scholarship of his day.

---

[17] Lowth, *De sacra poesie*, p. 39, 'profecto qui Metricam Hebraeam veram illam et genuinam instaurare conatur, is aedificium extruit, cui fundamentum in quo nitator plane deest'. English, vol. 1, p. 67.
[18] Lowth, *De sacra poesie*, p. 43 'qui in Historicis jam probe fuerit versatus, idem tamen in Poeticis sese plane hospitem sentiat, English, vol. 1, p. 75.

To assert that much of the prophetic literature was written in poetry was to go against the weight of traditional Jewish and Christian teaching. As noted earlier, the traditional Jewish punctuation of the Hebrew text recognised only Job, Psalms and Proverbs as poetic, while Jerome, who had translated the Bible from Hebrew into Latin, also denied that the prophets wrote in poetry; and for many hundreds of years Jerome's work provided the only knowledge of the Hebrew of the Bible in the Western Church.

Lowth argued that those whom God had called to be prophets had been trained in the art of poetry and music in a kind of college for potential prophets.[19] He appealed to the incident in 1 Samuel 10.10, where Saul encounters a band of prophets who cause him to prophesy. According to Lowth, this band of prophets had come down from the college where they were studying. Lowth also linked music to prophesying via the incident in 2 Kings 3.15, where a prophecy of Elisha is inspired by the playing of a minstrel. At 1 Chronicles 25.1 the names are given of temple musicians whose task was to prophesy with various musical instruments. Lowth claimed that the Hebrew word *nabi'*, normally rendered as 'prophet', 'equally denoted a Prophet, a Poet, or a Musician under the influence of divine inspiration'.[20] Modern scholarship would not accept Lowth's use of these passages and, in any case, he claimed too much for the passage about Saul meeting the prophets, when Lowth said that the prophets had come from the holy mountain of God, where the sacred college was situated. The passage does not say where the prophets had come from.

---

[19] Lowth, *De sacra poesie*, p. 225, English, vol. 2, pp. 11-12.
[20] Lowth, *De sacra poesie*, p. 226, designaret Prophetam, vel Poetam sive Musicum, divinitus incitatum, English, vol. 2, p. 14.

If Lowth had to resort to arguments that would not be acceptable to modern scholarship, this does not invalidate his conclusions. He was opposing the accumulated wisdom of centuries of Jewish and Christian learning, and in any case his use of scholarship conformed to that of his day, and needed to convince readers in the eighteenth century, not the twenty-first century. The convincing part of his argument was that many passages in the prophets were identical in form with those in the books acknowledged to be poetic – Job, Psalms and Proverbs – if one accepted Lowth's stress upon the importance of parallelism as a feature of biblical Hebrew poetry. Few modern scholars would disagree with Lowth on this matter, despite criticisms and refinements of his system.

Lowth distinguished between three main types of parallelism. In synonymous parallelism the same sentiment was repeated in different but equivalent terms. A good example is from Micah 6.6-8:

> Wherewith shall I come before JEHOVAH?
> Wherewith shall I bow myself unto the High God?
> Shall I come before him with burnt-offerings;
> With calves of a year old?
> Wil JEHOVAH be pleased with thousands of rams?
> With ten thousands of rivers of oil?
> Shall I give my first-born for my transgression?
> The fruit of my body for the sin of my soul?
> He hath shewed thee, O man, what is good:
> And what doth JEHOVAH require of thee,
> But to do justice, and to love mercy,
> And to be humble in walking with thy God?[21]

Lowth's second type of parallelism he called 'antithetic', because the main senses that were joined together were opposites. The form was particularly frequent in the Book of Proverbs (10.1):

---

[21] The example is taken from the English translation of the lectures, vol 2, p.21.

A wise son rejoiceth his father,
But a foolish son is the grief of his mother.[22]

Lowth cited two striking examples from Isaiah 54.7-8 and 65.13-14:

In a little anger have I forsaken thee;
But with great mercies will I receive thee again:
In a short wrath I hid my face for a moment from thee:
But with everlasting kindness will I have mercy on thee.[23]

Behold, my servants shall eat, but ye shall be famished;
Behold, my servants shall drink, but ye shall be thirsty:
Behold, my servants shall rejoice, but ye shall be confounded;
Behold, my servants shall sing aloud, for gladness of heart,
But ye shall cry aloud, for grief of heart.[24]

The third type of parallelism Lowth called 'synthetic' or 'constructive' parallelism and it is this category that has been most severely questioned and criticised by later scholarship. Lowth claimed that it was not characterised by sentences answering each other, as in synonymous parallelism, or opposing each other, as in antithetic parallelism, but by what he called the form of construction. An example of this is in Isaiah 58.5-8. Here the prophet describes the fast that is acceptable to God. It is to be noted that the grammatical forms of the words in the first three lines are similar: the verbs come first, the nouns second:

To dissolve the bands of wickedness;
To loosen the oppressive burdens;
To deliver those that are crushed by violence.[25]

---

[22] Lowth, *Isaiah*, p. xxiv.
[23] *Isaiah*, p. 174
[24] *Isaiah*, p. 206
[25] *Isaiah*, p. 185

I have given here only a bare outline of Lowth's arguments. In both the Lectures and the Preliminary Dissertation to *Isaiah* there are many more examples, including examples of how biblical Hebrew poetry in the prophetic books is built up into larger units. My aim in this lecture has been simply to introduce the main lines of his demonstration.

Robert Lowth changed the way we read the Bible and the way the Bible is printed. Although he has been criticised, his main claims have stood the test of time. In particular, he has changed the way we read the prophetic books of the Bible. Basic to the discussions that preceded his work, and which have followed it, is the question, 'What is biblical Hebrew poetry?' And this is part of the larger question, 'What is a poem and what is poetry?' I shall address these questions next week from the unusual angle of the philosophy of knowledge. That will lead us to the fundamental question that these lectures will address: Is it an accident that the Hebrew prophets delivered or wrote their messages in poetic form, or is it essential to their message? If they had used prose rather than poetry, would it have made any difference to their work? This is a question which, I believe, has not received in biblical scholarship the attention that it deserves. Is there something about the nature of poetry that makes biblical prophetic poetry the proper language for understanding God and God's word? These are the questions that we shall be exploring in the next four weeks.

LECTURE 2

The Poet Prophets of the Old Testament

What is poetry? We saw last week how Robert Lowth wrestled with this question in connection with his claim that the books of the prophets in the Old Testament were written largely in poetry. We saw how he used the alphabetic Psalms and similar compositions to work out what a line of biblical Hebrew poetry was, and how it was characterised by what he called parallelism. He established that biblical poetry did not rhyme. If it had metre, this was not recoverable, because how Hebrew was pronounced in biblical times had long been forgotten. However, the phenomenon of parallelism was sufficiently evident for it to be a means of identifying Hebrew poetry, along with the fact that the vocabulary of Hebrew poetry and its syntax were different from what was found in prose.

In today's lecture I propose to discuss the question, 'What is poetry?' from the angle of the philosophy of knowledge. In this I am deeply indebted to the work of the German philosopher Gerd Wolandt and to his book *Philosophie der Dichtung*.[26]

I begin with the following statement: 'The universe began with a big bang, since when the universe has been expanding'. Two questions arise. What does the statement mean, and in what sense is it true? The meaning of the statement depends on the fact that it belongs to the language of cosmology, and fits into physical descriptions of the nature and origin of the universe. Whether or not it is true depends on the findings of astronomers and physicists, the interpretation of these findings, and their formation into a theory that says that the universe began with a big bang that has caused the matter that makes up the universe to continue to accelerate away from this point of origin. However, it has to be added that anyone who accepts and advocates this theory will have to add the phrase 'to the best of our knowledge'. It may be that further research will modify or even disprove the theory. After all, the big bang theory is a comparatively recent one. I'm old enough to remember that before the big bang theory, the generally accepted view was that of Fred Hoyle and Hermann Bondi, known as 'the steady state theory'. What this means is that there must always be a provisionality about scientific statements. They must always leave open the possibility that further research will modify or disprove them.

The same is true of historical statements. It may be claimed that by letting Lenin return to Russia in 1917 the Germans were responsible for the Russian Revolution. Historians could challenge this by saying that it is too simplistic, or that the

---

[26] G. Wolandt, *Philosophie der Dichtung. Weltstellung und Gegenständlichkeit des poetischen Gedankens*, Berlin: de Gruyter, 1965.

revolution would have happened without Lenin, or that it might merely have taken a different form.

Poetry is quite different from scientific and historical statements. Take the following from Samuel Taylor Coleridge:

> When Evening's dusty car
> Crowned with her dewy star
> Steals o'er the fading sky in shadowy flight;
> On leaves of aspen trees
> We tremble to the breeze
> Veiled from the grosser ken of mortal sight.[27]

It is not immediately clear what this means, and interpreters might disagree. In other words, it is not located in language and forms of expression such as that found in astronomy or physics, which give sense to such terms as 'big bang' and 'expanding universe'. Secondly, it would not make sense to add to the poem the phrase 'to the best of our knowledge'. There is no way in which subsequent research would be able to modify or disprove what this poem is saying. Wolandt calls this feature of poetry *Abgeschlossenheit*, 'completedness'.[28] It is not possible to add anything to a poem; it possesses a completeness, whether or not it is considered to be a 'good' poem and or a 'bad' one.

In this connection Wolandt makes some interesting comments on drama as a form of poetry, noting that dramas such as Friedrich Schiller's *Wallenstein* and Johann Wolfgang Goethe's *Egmont* (and we could add the historical plays of Shakespeare), share with poetry this fact of completedness.[29] Schiller, Goethe and Shakespeare may well have made

---

[27] S. T. Coleridge, 'Songs of the Pixies V' in H. J. Jackson (ed.), *Samuel Taylor Coleridge*, Oxford: Oxford University Press, 1985, p. 8.
[28] Wolandt, p. 44.
[29] Wolandt, p. 58.

historical mistakes, (compare, for example, Shakespeare's portrayal of Joan of Arc as a sorceress in his play *Henry VI Part One*). But it is not the task of those who produce such dramas on the stage to try to correct the mistakes; and in any case, such corrections will themselves be liable to correction in the light of further research. The meaning of poetry is imminent or self-referential, that is, it does not have to appeal to anything outside itself to give it meaning or significance.

The next important feature of poetry to be discussed from the angle of the philosophy of knowledge is poetry as a way of thinking. That poetry is a way of thinking is emphasized by Wolandt. He writes: 'In poetry things are done and felt as in the primary world...The poem in its referential sense is thinking in the strict sense'.[30] It is important to consider how poetic thinking differs from empirical thinking. In empirical thinking we organize the sense impressions that come in upon us from the world around us, in binary or digital ways. Language, which plays a vital part in this process is, as we know from General Linguistics, itself a binary system. We organize the world into categories of opposites: dark/light, near/far, heavy/light, easy/difficult. Indeed, when we learn a new language it is valuable to begin with the words denoting opposites, such as this/that, here/there, up/down, entrance/exit. It is not generally appreciated that we have an excellent example of binary thinking in the opening chapter of the Book of Genesis where God separates light from darkness, day from night, creatures that fly from creatures that crawl, the earth from what is under the earth, and so on.

---

[30] Wolandt, pp. 176, 177, 'Im Gedicht wird gehandelt und gefühlt wie in der primären Welt ... Das Gedicht ist in seinen Verweisingssinn Denken im strengen Sinne'.

Poetic thinking is not binary in this way. Although poetry uses language which functions on binary principles, and draws upon the objects of our everyday experience and of the natural world for its subject matter, it combines these things together in ways which depend upon the individual imaginative genius or lack of it of the poets themselves. There is a splendid passage in Lowth's fifth lecture which sums up how the poetic genius takes the objects of the world and forms them into something quite different:

> The whole course of nature, this immense universe of things, offers itself to human contemplation, and affords an infinite variety, a confused assemblage, a wilderness, as it were, of images, which being collected in the materials of poetry, are selected and produced as occasion dictates. The mind of man is that mirror of Plato,[31] which as he turns about at pleasure, and directs to a different point of view, he creates another sun, other stars, planets, animals, and even another self. In this shadow or image of himself, which a man beholds when the mirror is turned inward towards himself, he is enabled in some degree to contemplate the souls of other men.[32]

In other words, poetry depicts the world around us in such a way as to create new perspectives, in which familiar things appear differently, things unconnected are brought together, meaning is imparted to what may seem pointless; and in all this, the human understanding of the world is changed, and

---

[31] See Plato's *Republic*, Book 10.
[32] Lowth, *De sacra poesie*, pp. 62-3, 'Omnis natura, immensa haec rerum universitas, humanae mentis contemplationi offertur atque objicitur; suppeditatque infinitam notionum varietatem, confusam quondam materiem atque sylvam, unde Imagines, veluti quaedam Poetica supellex, colliguntur, et delectu habito, prout usus fert, expromuntur, Animus hominis est illud Platonis Speculum, quod cum pro libitu undequaque circumfert, protinus solem alium efficit, alias stellas, terram, plantas, animalia, atque etiam seipsum. In hac sui ipsius umbra atque imagine, quam converso in se animi sui speculo homo intuetur, aliorum etiam hominum animos quodammodo inspicit.' English, vol.1, pp.116-17.

may be changed in such a way that behaviour and attitudes are affected. What we might loosely call 'the spiritual' comes into view in a way which may not be conveyed by empirical binary thinking.

One thing that is affected, and this is important for the present series of lectures, is how time functions in poetry, according to the philosophy of knowledge. In empirical thinking, time, divided into present, past and future, is an organising principle of our experience of the world around us. In poetic thinking it is different. The past and the future relate to the present by giving meaning to it, often by way of critique. It can criticise the present by depicting a past that was a Golden Age now lost, or it can speak of a coming New or Golden Age that will fulfil the disappointed hopes of the present. In both cases it may inspire people to work to improve the present in the light of poetic descriptions of the past and future. Wolandt remarks that in poetry the future gives meaning to the present, and that it is irrelevant whether that future comes to be realised or not.[33] Poets are not so much people who see into the future. They see into the present with insight that is special to them.

This matter must now be explored further with regard to the prophets of the Old Testament; for if they were poets, they did not see into the future but into their present; and if what Wolandt has said is correct, it does not matter whether what the prophets may have said about the future came to pass, or not. Yet in Christian tradition, certainly, the most important thing about the prophets is that they are believed to have foreseen the coming of Christ. Indeed, one of the standard

---

[33] Wolandt, p. 90.

Christian arguments for the inspiration of the Bible was that it contained a pattern of prophecy and fulfilment.

The Christian belief that the Old Testament prophets foresaw the coming of Jesus and his death and resurrection rests, in fact, upon hindsight, upon the fact that Jesus himself interpreted his work in terms of Old Testament passages in the prophetic books, and did so in a way that no one had done before. It must be stressed that this understanding of Jesus's mission was unique to himself. The reason why his followers and opponents did not understand who he was and what his mission was, was because no one reading the Old Testament scriptures in the time of Jesus read them in the way that he did. My late friend and colleague from Durham days, Professor C. K. Barrett, made it clear in an essay on the use of the Old Testament in the New Testament that this use was quite unique in the Judaism of the time of Jesus, and that this unique understanding can only have come from Jesus himself.[34] In Luke 24.25 the Risen Christ expounds to the two disciples on the Emmaus Road from the scriptures, beginning with Moses and all the prophets, 'the things concerning himself'. When the Early Church looked back to the Old Testament scriptures from the hindsight of the mission of Jesus, they saw how it could be understood in terms of the scriptures. I would want to say that this was possible, not because the prophets foresaw Jesus, but because the poet prophets spoke of their own present in such a way that they expressed profound insights that guided Jesus's own ministry, although he was the only one who knew this at the time.

---

[34] C. K. Barrett, 'The Interpretation of the Old Testament in the New' in P. R. Ackroyd, C. F. Evans, *The Cambridge History of the Bible, Vol. 1, From the Beginnings to Jerome*, Cambridge: Cambridge University Press, 1970, pp. 377-411.

But what, you might want to ask, about the Old Testament itself? Did it not regard the prophets as foretellers of the future? The answer is that prophets were certainly sometimes associated with what we would call soothsaying, but that increasingly the idea that prophets were forecasters of the future became so problematic that it was rejected. In 1 Samuel 9.6-9 Saul, who is looking for some lost asses, is advised to consult a man of God who has the reputation that what he says comes true. The comment is added that 'he who is now called a prophet was formerly called a seer'. However there are several incidents in the Old Testament which struggle to address the problem of how you tell a true prophet from a false one, if the nature of prophecy is to foretell the future. In 1 Kings 22, four hundred prophets who promise victory for King Jehoshaphat if he and his allies fight the Syrians at Ramoth-Gilead are opposed by one prophet, Micaiah, who predicts defeat and disaster. In Jeremiah 28, Jeremiah is directly opposed by another prophet named Hananiah. Hananiah predicts that God is about to defeat the Babylonians who have taken into exile King Jehoiachin. He asserts that the king will be restored to the throne in Jerusalem and that the temple vessels that were taken to Babylon will be returned. This is in direct contradiction to Jeremiah's view that no such imminent restoration will take place.

There is a strange and intriguing incident in 1 Kings 13 that deconstructs, as we would say today, the whole notion of predictive prophecy. A prophet goes to the altar at Bethel and prophesies its destruction. King Jeroboam orders him to be seized, whereupon the altar is mysteriously torn down and the king's hand is dried up. At the king's entreaty, the prophet restores his hand and in gratitude the king invites the prophet to come to his palace to be rewarded. The prophet refuses. God has forbidden him to eat or drink or to return home by the way that he came. Another prophet now chases after him and invites him into his house for refreshment. The first prophet refuses. God has commanded him not to eat or drink or to retrace his steps. The second prophet insists. He is also a prophet, he claims, and has been commanded by an angel to bring the first prophet to his home for refreshment. The first prophet gives in and goes to the house for refreshment. While they are eating, the second prophet who is providing the hospitality receives a word from God denouncing the first prophet for disobeying him by going to the house for refreshment. The first prophet sets off after the meal and is met and killed by a lion because of his disobedience. The passage points up the problem of how to know whether a prophet is speaking truly from God; and it is no accident that in one of the latest books of the Old Testament, Zechariah 13.3, we find the following passage, ironically enough in a prophetic book!

> I also will remove from the land the prophets and the unclean spirits. And if any one again appears as a prophet, his father and mother who bore him will say to him, you shall not live, for you speak lies in the name of the LORD.

If the Old Testament itself found the idea that prophets were primarily forecasters of the future problematic, how are we to proceed? We do so by going back to Jesus.

As I said earlier, it was a standard part of Christian proof that the Old Testament was inspired, that what the prophets had foreseen had been fulfilled in the coming of Jesus. Most of us will be familiar with Handel's oratorio *Messiah*, but will not realise the political and theological point that the libretto was trying to make.[35] In the eighteenth century, while Robert Lowth was arguing that the Old Testament prophets were poets, the Old Testament was being bitterly attacked by people we call Deists, who argued that the Old Testament was a barbaric book which should not be part of a Christian view of reality.[36] This was also an attack on the established Church of England. It had been reformed by Henry VIII and Edward VI, and their right to do this as kings had been justified by appeal to the examples of King David, who organized the temple worship, and Kings Hezekiah and Josiah, who had reformed the temple worship when it had been corrupted by Canaanite practices. To attack the Old Testament was to attack the Established Church, and one of the purposes of Handel's *Messiah* was to defend both the Old Testament and the Established Church by showing how the Old Testament prophecies about the Messiah has been fulfilled in Jesus. This is why *Messiah* begins where it does, with the voice crying in the wilderness of Isaiah chapter 40.1, a passage that relates directly to the ministry of John the Baptist at the beginning of the Gospel of Mark.

It is necessary for us to turn this reasoning upside down and to say that it is not the Old Testament prophets who validate Jesus, but that it is Jesus who validates the Old Testament prophets. Jesus needs no validation. He exemplifies what St Paul calls the 'foolishness of God', in which the Cross is folly to Greeks and a stumbling block to the Jews. Christians accept

---

[35] See R. Smith, *Handel's Oratorio Librettos and Eighteenth Century Thought*, Cambridge: Cambridge University Press, 1995.

[36] J. W. Rogerson, 'Writing the History of Israel in the 17th and 18th Centuries' in F. G. Martinez *et al.* (eds.), *The Scriptures and the Scrolls. Studies in Honour of A. S. van der Woude on the Occasion of his 65th Birthday*, Leiden: E. J. Brill, 1992, pp. 217-27, reprinted in J. W. Rogerson, *Cultural Landscapes and the Bible. Collected Essays*, Sheffield: Beauchief Abbey Press, 2014, pp. 303-315.

in faith that Jesus is the Servant of God and the Son of God. But if Jesus validates the prophets by seeing his own mission in terms of their words, he validates them not as foreseers of the future, but as poets who understand the present in such a profound way that their insights are valid for their own times and for future times and places. It will be one of my contentions in these lectures that Old Testament scholarship has devoted far too much attention to trying to date the Old Testament prophecies precisely, and far too little attention to what they say about the timeless and eternal present which embraces our own present also.

I want now to quote three passages from the book by Friedrich Gundolf on the German poet Stefan George (1868-1933), to whose inner circle Gundolf belonged. Gundolf's book is a work of art in itself, and claims powerfully that George was a prophet in the sense that is being considered in this lecture.[37] In the first quotation Gundolf was replying to a criticism of George, a criticism that could be equally applied to the Old Testament prophets, that George's denunciations of what he regarded as ugly and blind in the society of his day was simply disillusionment. It was not disillusionment, argued Gundolf, but was born of a vision of hope that George entertained:

> The negative judgements of Hölderlin and Nietzsche are misunderstood when they are taken to be the complaints of malcontent. All curses and denials of prophets take their meaning from an unconditional 'Yes' demanded by the appearance of a new god. Without meaning to, each 'Yes' entails a 'No', each eternity necessarily creates mere time; every beginning an end; every space, limits; every height a depth. But it is the prophets, those who proclaim new gods, i.e., people of the turning point (*Wende*) whose

---

[37] F. Gundolf, *George*, Berlin: Georg Bondi, 1930, 3rd ed. of the 1920 book.

'Yes' is at the same time reproof and judgement, and appears to a self-satisfied generation to be no more than deniers so long as their new god, their new 'Yes', is not recognised [my translation]. [38]

The second quotation concerns George's remarkable poem 'The Antichrist', and here Gundolf compares George to the writer of the Book of Revelation, when he refers to the vision from Patmos. His summary of the poem is itself a powerful piece of poetic writing, arguably even more powerful than George's own diagnosis of the corrupting power of evil in society. It was written over 90 years ago, and if it sounds uncomfortably relevant to today's world of post-truth and post-facts, this is because it is prophetic, i.e., it speaks of a present that is eternally being judged:

'The Antichrist' is the gigantic final form of a secularised national life that perverts every truth, soothes every anxiety and sucks the blood from every reason. The falsifier, the dazzler, the ensnarer, the mis-user, the confuser, the 'prince of vermin', who makes what is difficult, pleasant and cheap for everyone; who corrupts what exists, perverts the arts, bends the standards, falsifies what is true – the demon of corruption, the herald of disaster, hedged between flabby nature and lustful spirit. The abolition of Christianity, the degenerate spirit and world of souls has found here a mighty unveiling (*Apokalypse*), as in the vision from Patmos of the fall of the heathen world of blood and sensuality. This poem alone would put George in the ranks of the great prophets. It

[38] F. Gundolf, p. 221, 'Man mißversteht sie ebenso wie die Gedichte Hölderlins und Nietzsches, wenn man sie als die Anklagen eines Mißvergnügten nimmt. Erst, von dem unbedingten Ja aus, von dem Erscheinen eines neuen Gottes, der fordert, haben alle Flüche und Verneinungen der Propheten ihren Sinn. Ganz unwillkürlich setzt jedes neue Ja sein Nein, ganz unausweichlich schafft jede Ewigkeit eine bloße Zeit, jeder Beginn ein Ende, jeder Raum Grenzen und jede Höhe eine Tiefe. Aber es sind die Profeten, die Künder neuer Götter, also Menschen der Wende, deren Ja zugleich Rüge und Gericht wird, und die einem ganzen selbstgefälligen Zeitalter als Verneiner vorkommen, so-lang man ihren neuen Gott, ihr neues Ja noch nicht wahrnimmt'.

has nothing to compare with it for its visionary flight, its dark greatness, its plastic energy and thundering distance [my translation].[39]

The final quotation can also be applied to the Old Testament prophets with little alteration:

Nations are first created by gods ... this has been known by every seer from biblical times to Hölderlin, and has named the god together with the nation ... Such a seer ... feels the coming fate of the nation most intensely, for in the new god everything is there that he brings and demands. Being a seer is only the present receiving of his outpouring light which only reaches the darker distant places later ... It is less a seeing in advance of what will happen in the future and more an immediate discerning of what is already on its way [my translation].[40]

I have been arguing that poet prophets do not see the future but the present, but the present as time eternally present. There is one more question to be asked. Do the poet prophets see in the present that is eternally present, an eternity beyond time? Is their view restricted to the world of time and space, or

---

[39] Gundolf, p. 232, "'Der Widerchrist' ist die gigantische Endgestalt des entgotteten Völkerlebens, die jede Wahrheit umkehrt, jedes Gesetz umgeht, jeden Quell trübt und jeden Grund aussaugt ... der Fälscher, der Blender, der Umgarner, der Mißbraucher, der Wirrer, "der Fürst des Geziefers", der das Schwere bequem und billig-massenhaft macht, das Wesen nach-scheint, die Künste vor-täuscht, das Grade biegt das Ächte ersetzt – der Dämon des Schwindels, der Vorbote des Untergangs, geheckt zwischen der schlaffen Natur und dem geilen Geist. Die Endschaft der Christenheit, die entartete Geist – und Seelenwelt hat hier eine weniger ein Vorhersehen dessen was eintreffen wird als ein Zuerst-spüren dessen was da oder unterwegs ist'.

[40] Gundolf, p. 242, 'Erst durch Götter werden Völker geschaffen ... das hat von den biblischen Zeiten bis zu Hölderlin jeder Seher gewußt, und den Gott mit dem Volk zusammen aufgerufen. Ein solcher fühlt auch am eignen Leib ... am unmittelbarsten die kommenden Geschicke des Volkes ... denn im neuen Gott ist alles schön da was er bringt und fordert. Sehertum ist nur der gegen-wärtige Empfang seiner Strahlung, welche die Dumpferen Ferneren erst später erreicht weniger ein Vorhersehen dessen was eintreffen wird als ein Zuerst-spüren dessen was da oder unterwegs ist'.

do they see, and grasp, and are they grasped by, a reality that is beyond the world?

Perhaps it is no accident that when St Paul tries to describe the secret and hidden wisdom of God in 1 Corinthians 2.9, he quotes a fragment of Hebrew prophetic poetry, from Isaiah 64.4:

> Eye hath not seen,
> Nor ear heard,
> Neither have entered into the heart of man,
> The things which God hath prepared for them that love
> him.

We note the parallelism of the three lines; we also note that, from the standpoint of empirical thinking, Paul says nothing. He makes three negative statements; but from the standpoint of poetry the fragment says a great deal, and does so by invoking what we may call the sublime.

The sublime can be thought of in the first instance as the human reaction to phenomena of nature, such as an amazing sunset, or a massive waterfall, or the grandeur of snow-capped mountains that make an overwhelming impression upon the observer. We are not able to grasp these experiences with the binary mechanisms of thought and language that I mentioned earlier. For this reason, they may make us react with fear, or with awe and wonder; they may make us aware of our insignificance as human beings. They may make us aware of our mortality, and by stripping away our self-confidence and self-sufficiency, the experiences may make us sense the eternal, they may give us intimations of an unseen world to which in a mysterious way we feel we may belong.

That there is a link between poetry and the sublime has been observed since the writings of a first century AD unknown writer named, for convenience, Longinus; and there is a reference to Longinus and the sublime in Lowth's fourteenth lecture.[41] There, he links the sublime with passionate outpourings of Hebrew poetic compositions. For our purposes, we can say that sublime poetry is an attempt to express in words the overwhelming impression made by our experience of the sublime, experience that can strip us of our certainties and make us contemplate realities beyond our world of time and space. In the Bible, the supreme example of this is in the final chapters of the Book of Job (38-42) where God speaks to Job out of a whirlwind and puts before him not only the awe-inspiring phenomena of the world but also some seemingly trivial instances. Confronted with the sublime, Job confesses that

> I have heard of thee with the hearing of the ear; but now mine eye seeth thee. Wherefore I abhor myself, and repent in dust and ashes. (Job 42.5-6)

Perhaps I can add that in today's world, if we see, for example, a great waterfall, such as the Rhinefall at Schaffhausen, we photograph it. Earlier generations would have tried to paint it, or to express the experience in poetry. But it is not only the sublime that can have this effect upon us. Beauty can act in the same way, and there is a remarkable passage in the didactic novel by the nineteenth-century German philosopher Jakob Friedrich Fries, entitled *Julius und Evagoras*, which expresses this fact. Fries was a profound student of Immanuel Kant and sought, in his own writings, to go beyond Kant, especially in the area of aesthetics. For Fries, experience of the beautiful is experience of the eternal values

---

[41] Lowth, *De sacra poesie*, p. 167, English, vol. 1, p. 307.

of truth and harmony; and such experiences can best be described in poetry:

> The power of beauty in the life of man ought to awaken our intuitive awareness of the ideas of the eternally true essence of things, an intuitive awareness or presentiment which animates faith within the sphere of human knowledge…In addition to the ordinary view of things, which is based on understanding, there is, within our spirit, yet another view of the world – a higher and a transfigured view of the world, which belongs to religion and beauty. This transfigured view of the world has, in the ideas of beauty, its own higher right to truth, so to speak. This truth is distinct from the truth of the understanding, which dominates the sciences. The truth of beauty is the torch which lights the man inspired with enthusiasm, is the torch which lights the man of devotion, and all those who dedicate, or strive to make the sacrifice of, their temporal existence to eternal ideas.[42]

Poets, then, encountering in the sublime and the beautiful, intimations of an eternal world, give expression in their poetry to these intuitions, and enable us to see in their work not only profound understandings of the present, but intuitions of what lies beyond time and space.

---

[42] J. F. Fries, *Julius und Evagoras. Ein philosophischer Roman*, Göttingen: Vandenhoeck & Ruprecht, 1910, p. 105, 'Das sollte die Macht der Schönheit im Leben des Menschen ein, dass sie für die Ideen des ewig wahren Wesens der Dinge eine Ahndung erwecke, welche den Glauben in der menschlichen Erkenntnis lebendig macht … Es ist in unserem Geiste neben der gemeinen verständigen Ansicht der Dinge noch eine andere höhere verklärte Weltansicht, welche der Religion und der Schönheit gehört. Diese hat in den Ideen der Schönheit gleichsam nur ihr höheres Recht der Wahrheit des Verstandes, welche die Wissenschaften beherrscht. Die Wahrheit der Schönheit ist es, deren Fackel dem Begeisterten leuchtet und den Andächtigen und denen, welche all ihr zeitliches Dasein ewigen Ideen zu weihen oder aufopfern streben'. English translation in D. Z. Phillips (ed.), Jakob Friedrich Fries, *Dialogues on Morality and Religion*, Oxford: Basil Blackwell, 1982, p. 79.

It will be my task in the fourth lecture to illustrate this by interpreting the so-called Servant Songs in the later chapters of the Book of Isaiah. Next week, I shall consider how the Old Testament prophets performed and delivered their messages in public.

LECTURE 3

The Forms of Old Testament Prophecy

The Old Testament prophets were not only poets, they were performers. Indeed, as poets, they had to be performers, for only by being performers could they convey their poetry to the people they needed to reach. In ancient Israel and Judah, the skills of reading and writing were mostly the preserve of the scribes who were employed by the royal court and the temple, and who had been trained at a scribal school. Furthermore, the lack of any kind of writing materials for general use meant that most ordinary people had no occasion or need to read and write. If it was necessary to have legal documents drawn up, for example, to prove ownership of land, this was done by scribes, just as today we would use a solicitor to produce a similar legal document. When the prophets delivered their messages to ordinary people, they did this orally; and in order to gain attention and an audience, they used various devices to draw attention to themselves.

In Jeremiah chapter 27 the prophet is commanded to take thongs and yoke-bars, and to wear them on his neck. This, clearly, would draw attention to him. He is to do this as a sign to the envoys of various local small nations who have come to Jerusalem to consult with King Zedekiah. These are the envoys of the kings of Edom, Moab, Ammon, Tyre and Sidon. The message that Jeremiah is to convey is that all these nations will become subject to Nebuchadnezzar the king of Babylon. In order to avoid disaster, those nations will need to put their necks under the yoke of the king of Babylon, otherwise disaster will come upon them.

In Jeremiah chapter 19 the prophet is told to go and to buy an earthen flask and to go with it and some of the elders and senior priests to the valley of the son of Hinnom. This is the place where the rubbish was burned in ancient Jerusalem. When the prophet has delivered his message, he is to break the flask in the sight of his listeners and to say that the city and its inhabitants and its houses will be broken in the way that the flask has been broken, because of the disobedience of the people of Judah and Jerusalem, and their refusal to hear God's words through the prophets.

In the First Book of Kings, chapter 11, the prophet Ahijah takes a new garment which he is wearing and tears it into 12 pieces. He gives ten pieces to Jeroboam, who will later lead a revolt of the northern tribes against the son of Solomon, Rehoboam. This symbolises the fact that the united kingdom of David and Solomon will be divided, that Jeroboam will have ten of the twelve tribes, and that only two will be left to the house of David.

An older generation of Old Testament scholarship that did not understand the nature of symbolic actions tended to describe incidents such as these as instances of magic or magical beliefs, with the physical action being believed to put into effect the words that were being spoken. We now know much more about symbolic actions, and are on safer ground if we assume that the symbolic actions had the main purpose of attracting an audience to hear the prophet's words. The incidents that I have described are relatively straightforward, but there are some complicated ones that call for further explanation. Before I consider them, however, I want to refer to another incident in the Book of Jeremiah which indicates the oral nature of the messages of the prophets, how they reached an audience, and how they came to be written down.

In the year 605 BC, the prophet Jeremiah was instructed by God to dictate to his secretary, Baruch, the words of prophecy which Jeremiah had spoken up to that point. Because Jeremiah was debarred from going to the temple (we do not know exactly why), Jeremiah instructed Baruch to go to the temple on a fast day when many people would be coming to the temple in connection with the fast. Baruch was to read out to all the people who were there the words that Jeremiah had dictated, and he did so in the following year, 604 BC: 'Baruch read Jeremiah's words aloud in the temple in the chamber of Gemariah the son of Shaphan the secretary, in the upper court at the entry of the New Gate of the Lord's house' (Jeremiah 36.1-10).

One of the sons of Gemariah went to the royal palace and informed the nobles who were there, of what was going on. The nobles sent word that Baruch and the scroll should be brought to them. Baruch came and read it to them, whereupon they decided that it was necessary for the king, Jehoiakim, to know what had happened. They also wanted to know from where Baruch had got the scroll, to which he replied that Jeremiah had dictated it. The nobles told Baruch and Jeremiah to go into hiding. The group now proceeded to the king's court where they reported to the king what had gone on. The king ordered that the scroll should be read in his presence. We are told that it was the ninth month, which probably means that it was autumn, and that the king was sitting in his winter house in front of a fire burning in a brazier. As the scroll was read to him, the king took a penknife and cut off each portion of the scroll after it had been read, and threw it into the brazier until the entire scroll had been consumed by the fire. We are told that none of those who heard what was in the scroll showed any kind of remorse or emotion. The king ordered that Jeremiah and Baruch should be brought to him, but they could not be found.

So far, I have mentioned cases of performance that can easily be understood. I now turn to ones that, on the face of it, are puzzling. In Isaiah chapter 21.2 the prophet is instructed to loose the sackcloth from his loins and to remove his sandals from his feet. It is explained the prophet had been walking naked and barefoot for three years. The interpretation of this is not easy. 'Naked' does not mean literally without any clothes on; and exactly how the three years would be reckoned or counted by those who observed Isaiah's behaviour is unclear. However, there is sufficient in the passage to indicate that Isaiah had been dressing in an unusual way that would draw the attention to him of the people among whom he lived. We are told that he was to do this as a sign that the king of Assyria would take captive the Egyptians, so that the unusual dress of the prophet would resemble that of Egyptians being marched into exile. Whether or not the king of Assyria did in fact defeat Egypt at this time is much discussed in the scholarly literature. For our present purposes it is sufficient to say that the passage indicates that Isaiah drew attention to himself by means of dressing strangely.

In Jeremiah 25 the prophet is told to take from God's hand a cup of the wine of wrath and to cause a number of kings to drink from it. I shall not bother to list all the names of the kings that are mentioned in the text, except to say that last of all the king of Babylon is to drink. The prophet is to do this as a sign of the judgement of God that is to come upon these nations. The difficulty in the passage is obvious. How is the prophet going to cause the kings of nations from as far afield as Egypt, Arabia, Tyre and Sidon, and Babylon to drink from his cup? For the moment, I shall leave the question unanswered and turn to some other problematic examples.

In Ezekiel 4 the prophet is told to take a piece of brick and to draw a picture of Jerusalem upon it and to portray siege works and battering rams so that people who see the brick will see it as a sign that Jerusalem will undergo a siege. Then he is to lie upon his left side for the number of the days of the punishment of Israel, a period of 390 days, symbolising 390 years. Once he has completed the 390 days he is to lie on his right side as a sign of the punishment of the house of Judah, in which position he is to lie for forty days, symbolising 40 years. Also, he is to wear or be bound by ropes, which will prevent him from turning from one side to the other, until the appointed days have been completed. As in the case of Isaiah going about with usual clothes for a period of three years, we have to ask the question how people would know that 390 days and 40 days had passed? People did not have diaries and the keeping and recording of dates was difficult in the ancient world. Who was to feed Ezekiel while he was lying on his side? How would he discharge his natural functions if he was tied up so that he could not move? We seem to be faced with an impossibility, and yet we must not reach the conclusion that these things did not really happen and that they are simply made up as part of a story.

The best solution to these questions was provided some years ago by the German Old Testament scholar Bernhard Lang, although a similar suggestion had been made some years earlier by the Israeli scholar Yehezkel Kaufmann. Lang suggested that what we have here are instances of what he called street theatre. The scenes described in Isaiah and Jeremiah and Ezekiel are to be acted out, so that although they are not literally true, they are true in the sense that performances were given that conveyed a message, but which above all set the scene for prophets to deliver their messages to those assembled. Lang defines it as

> The performance of street theatre in which the prophet illustrates his word by game, mime and props. Isaiah warns of an anti-Assyrian league by appearing in the loincloth of a prisoner of war...Jeremiah buys a big stone jar, smashes it to pieces at Jerusalem's Gate of the Potsherds and throws it on to the rubbish dump...Ezekiel acts out the besieging of Jerusalem and enters into a form of hunger strike, eating only bad food in small rations, to demonstrate that a shortage of foodstuffs is to be expected...One should not underestimate the provocative effect of such a demonstration in a society which knows of no mass media...the prophets mean to cause a sensation and to challenge a wider public to take a stand. It is the street theatre itself which teaches us to understand the prophets not only as theologians of a meditative bent, but also as showmen, as experts in public agitation and propaganda.[43]

I would want to add that it was also a way of gathering an audience for the prophets to deliver their message in poetry.

Before I leave the subject of street theatre I want to comment on another passage from a prophetic book and how it may

---

[43] B. Lang, *Monotheism and the Prophetic Minority* (Social World of Biblical Antiquity Series, 1), Sheffield: Almond Press, 1983, pp. 81-2.

best be understood as a dramatization. This brings us back to the Israeli scholar Yehezkel Kaufmann and his monumental work in modern Hebrew *The Religion of Israel*.[44] The passage is Hosea chapters 1-3. The book begins with a passage that has vexed interpreters for centuries. The prophet is instructed to

> take a wife of harlotry and to have children of harlotry.

What does this mean? Some interpreters were troubled by the idea that God could tell the prophet to do something sinful, that is, to marry a prostitute. Another problem is the meaning of the phrase 'children of harlotry'. Even if Hosea's wife had been a prostitute, the children would be legitimately born, so how could they be children of harlotry, unless they were to be encouraged by the prophet to engage in the promotion and practice of prostitution. (There are two sons and a daughter). This seems unlikely.

Something of the difficulty is seen by the way in which the great Puritan scholar and commentator, Matthew Poole, handled the passage. He suggests that if the wife, who is named Gomer, had formerly been a prostitute, she ceased to be so on being married to Hosea. The phrase 'children of harlotry' may refer to children who had been born to Gomer while she was a prostitute, before her marriage, children who were now accepted into the family by the prophet. Unfortunately, the text rules out such an explanation when it states clearly that 'she conceived and bore him a son'.

In Hosea chapter 3 the prophet is instructed to

---

[44] Y. Kaufmann, Toldot HaEmunah HaYisraelit, Tel Aviv: Devir, 1964, vol. 3, part 1, pp. 102-103.

> Love a woman who is beloved of a paramour and is an
> adulteress.

The prophet buys her for 15 shekels of silver and a quantity of barley and says to her,

> You must dwell as mine for many days; you shall not play
> the harlot or belong to another man.

Poole argues that this woman cannot be the prophet's wife mentioned in the first chapter, to whom Hosea is still married. This second, previously unmarried, woman is to live with him; not to be married with him.[45]

In the nineteenth century a theory emerged that became widespread in religious education in Britain after the Second World War. It supposed that, taken together, chapters 1-3 of Hosea were biographical. Hosea had married a woman named Gomer, and had had two sons and a daughter. She then left him and became a prostitute. After a period of time he rediscovered her working as a slave, and bought her out of slavery for 15 shekels of silver. Out of this personal tragedy the prophet came to know something of God's love for a chosen people that had turned away from his love to the carnal delights of the religion of Baal and its sacred prostitution.

Although this is a very moving and attractive interpretation, there is nothing in the actual text of Hosea to support it, and it leaves unexplained the perplexing phrases 'wife of harlotry' and 'children of harlotry'. Further, it does not explain another point that I have not yet mentioned, that when the prophet's children are born he gives them symbolic names. The first son

---

[45] M. Poole, *A Commentary on the Holy Bible* (1700), Edinburgh: Banner of Truth, 1962, pp. 850-3, 857.

is named 'Jezreel' as a sign that the house of the Israelite king Jehu will be punished. The daughter is named 'not pitied' (*lo ruchamah*), because God will no longer have pity on Israel and Judah. The second son is named 'not my people' (*lo 'ammi*) as a sign that God is turning his back on his people. These namings are similar to the other symbolic actions that have been mentioned, such as Jeremiah wearing a yoke or smashing the jar, and Kaufmann's suggestion that this is all theatrical and dramatic makes sense. The prophet, his wife and his children act out a drama in which Gomer plays the role of a prostitute (presumably by her dress and gestures) and the children are given the symbolic names that underpin the prophet's message. Kaufmann, rightly in my view, sees no connection between chapter 1 and chapter 3 of Hosea.

The consideration of street theatre raises an interesting question to which there cannot be a decisive answer, but which is worth raising. I shall shortly show how prophets used forms of speech such as love songs and funeral dirges to present their messages. In the passages that I shall cite there is no mention of the prophets wearing any special clothing, but one wonders if the funeral dirge was delivered while the prophet was wearing sackcloth and ashes or the love song was delivered in dress appropriate to wooing or a wedding.

The love song that I want to discuss comes in Isaiah 5, and I give it in Robert Lowth's translation:

> Let me sing now a song to my Beloved;
> A song of loves concerning his vineyard.
> My Beloved had a vineyard,
> On a high and fruitful hill:
> And he fenced it round, and he cleared it from stones,
> And he planted it with the vine of Sorek;
> And he built a tower in the midst of it,

And he hewed out also a lake therein:
And he expected, that it should bring forth grapes,
But it brought forth poisonous berries.
And now, O inhabitants of Jerusalem,
And ye men of Judah,
Judge, I pray you, between me and my vineyard:
What could have been done more to my vineyard,
Than I have done to it?
Why, when I expected that it should bring forth grapes,
Brought it forth poisonous berries?
But come now, and I will make known unto you,
What I purpose to do to my vineyard:
To remove its hedge, and it shall be devoured;
To destroy its fence, and it shall be trodden down.
And I will make it a desolation;
It shall not be pruned, neither shall it be digged;
But the briar and the thorn shall spring up in it;
And I will command the clouds,
That they shed no rain upon it.
Verily, the vineyard of JEHOVAH God of hosts is the house
of Israel:
And the men of Judah the plant of his delight:
And he looked for judgment, but behold tyranny:
And for righteousness, but behold the cry of the oppressed.

In view of what I said earlier about the possibility of the prophet wearing appropriate clothing when delivering this message, it is noteworthy that Bernhard Duhm suggests that the prophet is wearing the mask of a folk singer, which he removes when he gets to the point of challenging his hearers to come to a decision.[46] A generally-held view connects the passage with the kind of speech that the friend of a bridegroom might make at a wedding. We can think in our own culture of the best man at a wedding, telling the assembled guests about the bridegroom.

---

[46] B. Duhm, *Das Buch Jesaia*, Göttingen: Vandenhoeck & Ruprecht, 46th ed., 1922, p.54.

The speaker describes how the friend chose an excellent location for his vineyard, made the very best preparations for its soil and protection from wild animals and thieves, and planted the best variety of grapes possible. The meaning of the words rendered by Lowth as 'vine of Sorek' assumes that the plants came from the valley of Sorek, south of Jerusalem, which was renowned for the quality of its grapes. Today's scholarship connects the name with words in the Semitic languages for redness, and suggests that a variety of red grape is indicated. The Hebrew word translated by Lowth as 'poisonous berries' may be connected with a verb that means to smell or stink,[47] or it may be a weed that resembles a vine.[48]

At this point the speaker changes from the friend to the owner of the vineyard and asks the listeners to make a judgement. The procedure is similar to what happens with some of the parables (cp. The Good Samaritan). What would they, the listeners, do, given that the hopes of the husbandman had been so cruelly disappointed? At this stage, we must remember that we are dealing with prophetic poetry, not viticulture. There could be several ways of dealing with the problem that the best grapes had produced something worthless. For example, one could try planting a different variety of grape. To demolish the whole vineyard, to let it be trampled by wild beasts, to make it suffer drought, and produce thorns and briars seems to be far too drastic, and perhaps the listeners were expected to feel like that. What began as a song praising a friend had turned into something very provocative.

---

[47] H. Wildberger, *Jesaja* (Biblischer Kommentar Altes Testament x/i), Neukirchen-Vluyn: Neukirchene Verlag, 1972, p. 169.
[48] M. Zohari, 'bᵉushim' in *Enzyklopedia Hamiqrait*, vol. 2, Jerusalem: Bialik Institute, 1954, pp. 9-10.

The climax arrives as the prophet applies the song to his listeners. Whatever they may have thought of the drastic action of the husbandman, God, by implication, is determined to make a desolation of his people that they may well think is completely uncalled for. The grapes and the poisonous berries are now given a meaning; and in doing this, the prophet uses word-play which is apparent, even given our scanty knowledge of how Hebrew was pronounced. God looked for judgment (*mishpat*) and what resulted was tyranny (*mispach*); he looked for righteousness (*sedaqah*), but what came was oppression (*seaquah*).

At this point it may be well to recall the quotation I used last week from Friedrich Gundolf's book on Stefan George, to the effect that George was not simply a man disillusioned with his world. His 'no' came from a mighty 'yes' as he saw a vision of hope. The same is true here. The part of the poem that speaks of the careful preparation of the vineyard points to God's work in bringing the Israelites from slavery and planting them in a land 'flowing with milk and honey'. The purpose of this was not to provide a dwelling place where the Israelites could enjoy a comfortable life. The aim was to create a people that embodied in its social interactions the graciousness that God had shown in redeeming and establishing the people. God looked for judgment and justice, but did not find them. Isaiah is not a secular liberal humanist who opposes inequality and exploitation. He is a prophet of the kingdom of justice and righteousness that God, the creator of the universe, has established. He is the herald of a hope that in obedience to God an ideal society can be created. The behaviour of the people is not an offence against human decency. It is an offence against God, who has established the vineyard. The 'yes' that God had spoken to his people in establishing them created the 'no' which was the people's answer to him, and to each other. The passage was originally heard by an audience that was at first intrigued and then provoked by it. As it has come down to us it can be read at a much deeper level than was possible for those who first heard it.

I turn from a love song to a funeral dirge, found at the beginning of Amos 5. Here it is in my translation of verses 1-5:

> Hear this word which I lift up against you as a
> lamentation, O house of Israel.
> Fallen, no more to rise up
> is virgin Israel.
> She lies prostrate on her land;
> No one helps her up.
> For thus says the Lord GOD:
> The city from which a thousand went
> Will retain only a hundred,
> And from the one from which a hundred went
> Will only ten remain [for the house of Israel].
> For thus says the LORD to the house of Israel:
> Seek me; then you shall live.
> Do not seek Beth-el'
> Do not go to Gilgal
> [nor pass to Beersheba],
> Gilgal will surely be taken captive
> [Hebrew: *haGilgal galoh yigleh*]
> And Beth-el will become (Beth)-Aven.

We have seen in these lectures that there is disagreement among scholars as to whether we can recover Hebrew metre, but according to many commentators, Amos 5.2-3 is an example of Qinah or lament rhythm, in which a line of five stresses is divided into a three, followed by a two. In my translation I have tried to indicate this. 'Fallen no more to rise up' represents three stresses, and 'is virgin Israel' represents two. It has been further suggested that this 'three-two pattern' imitated a limping dance that was performed at funerals. It is possible, then, that the prophet was wearing dress suitable for mourning, and that he delivered his message singing a funeral dirge and performing a limping dance.

The Hebrew verbs at the beginning of the first and second lines of the lamentation (translated as 'fallen' and 'prostrate') are in what we call the 'completed aspect', that is, they describe the things as completed, whether or not they have yet happened or are likely to happen. Completed and pending aspects are features of modern Slavonic languages such as Russian and Polish, as well as some forms of modern Arabic. The prophet is not describing a past event, nor is he predicting a coming one. He is seeing reality in a special way.

The phrase 'virgin Israel' is meant to convey the idea of a young life cut brutally short before it has had the chance to fulfil its potential or to beget offspring. In our gender-conscious age we might ask why it is 'virgin Israel' and not 'young man Israel'. The answer is that in Hebrew, nations are feminine and that it would be as odd in Hebrew to speak of 'young man Israel' as it would be in English to speak of 'mother time' or 'father earth'. The young woman's plight is such that even as she lies on her own territory, not foreign land, she has no helper. Such is the fate, or better, the condition, of the nation as the prophet sees it.

The imagery turns to that of warfare. The terms 'thousand', 'hundred' and 'ten' refer to military units, not actual numbers of soldiers, but a major disaster is envisaged as a way of describing the state of the people. The prophet does not necessarily have any imminent military campaign in view, but the military language about loss of life is appropriate for a funeral address.

There is a ray of hope in this darkness. The prophet speaks in God's name. 'Seek me, then you shall live'. Life is a gift of God, not merely in a biological sense, but as it embraces social relationships. Bethel and Gilgal were sanctuaries which Amos's hearers might well visit on pilgrimages. Their drawback for the prophet was that such pilgrimages might give to the people a false sense of security, the feeling that because they had made the pilgrimages, their future prosperity was secured. The prophet makes puns upon the names of the sanctuaries to show that they are human institutions and therefore impermanent. The pun on Gilgal, (*haGilgal galoh yigleh*) is striking. The pun on Beth-el depends on the fact that Beth-el means 'house of God' while Beth-aven would mean something like 'house of evil'.

What, in this case, does 'seek me' (seek God) mean? This is not a plea for the Israelites to go to an alternative sanctuary such as Jerusalem. It is rather that God's voice can be heard through the prophets, the prophets who speak of God the creator and lord of the universe, who has called Israel into a special relationship with himself in order to be a light to the nations.[49] There is a strong contrast in the funeral address between life and death. Life comes from hearing and obeying God's word through the prophets. Death comes from ignoring their voice and from believing that outward religious observances such as pilgrimages can take the place of reliance on God's living word and obedience to it. Like the love song in Isaiah 5, the funeral dirge in Amos 5 reveals depths of significance to those of us who can read and study it today.

---

[49] See the discussion in J. Jeremias, *Der Prophet Amos* (Das Alte Testament Deutsch 24, 2), Göttingen: Vandenhoeck & Ruprecht, 1995, pp. 65-6.

I want to conclude by referring briefly to the so-called messenger formula. This was a convention which kings used in the ancient world to convey messages to each other. Claus Westermann has traced it as far back as the third millennium BC city of Mari on the Euphrates river, in the north-east of Syria close to the border with Iraq.[50] What I shall say this evening is an over-simplification of Westermann's extensive discussion, but will indicate the main points as they affect this lecture on the Old Testament prophets.

Generally speaking, the method used by rulers to convey messages to each other began with the ruler who was sending the message speaking it orally in the presence of the messenger or ambassador who was to take it to the ruler who was to receive it. When the messenger came into the presence of the receiving ruler he repeated verbatim the message that he had heard spoken by the sending ruler. Westermann traces the formal structure that the message came to take. The sending king would identify himself, would name the ruler who was to receive the message, would add a kind of preamble describing why the message was being sent, and would then state the message.

There is an example of this in the Book of Judges (11.13-28) when the judge Jephthah and the king of the Ammonites send messages to each other prior to beginning hostilities against each other. Jephthah wants to know why the Ammonite king is hostile. The king replies that the Israelites occupied Ammonite territory during their journey from Egypt to Canaan, and they must now return it peacefully or expect war.

---

[50] C. Westermann, *Basic Forms of Prophetic Speech*, London: Lutterworth Press, 1967, pp. 98-163.

Jephthah replies, and here we get part of the messenger formula:

> Jephthah sent messengers again to the king of the
> Ammonites and said to him, Thus says Jephthah (v.14).

There then follows a long account of what happened when the Israelites were on their journey from Egypt, and how, when various kings would not allow passage to the Israelites through their territory, they had to resort to force to proceed on their journey. The occupation of Ammonite land was accidental, but it was also decreed by God. After this preamble, the main message follows, introduced by the word 'therefore':

> I therefore have not sinned against you and you do me
> wrong by making war on me (v.27).

What we see in this account is the self-identification of the sender of the message ('Thus says Jephthah'), the preamble, and the message introduced by 'therefore'. When we look at the Book of Jeremiah in particular, we see a prophet using this formula, with the difference that the prophet is not a messenger from another ruler to the king of Judah; he is a messenger from God. The implication is that the prophet has stood in the court of God, and is now repeating the message that he heard God speak! A good example comes in the incident that I related earlier, when Jeremiah's scroll is cut up by King Jehoiakim and burned in the brazier. The following word comes from God to the prophet:

> Thus saith the LORD:
> Thou hast burned this roll, saying, Why hast thou written
> therein, saying, The king of Babylon shall certainly come
> and destroy this land, and shall cause to cease from thence
> man and beast?

Therefore thus saith the LORD of Jehoiakim king of Judah: He shall have none to sit upon the throne of David: and his dead body shall be cast out in the day to the heat, and in the night to the frost.

And I will punish him and his seed and his servants for their iniquity; and I will bring upon them, and upon the inhabitants of Jerusalem, and upon the men of Judah, all the evil that I have pronounced against them; but they hearkened not. (Jeremiah 36.29-31)

The messenger formula, with its implication that the prophet had come hot-foot from the very presence of God to convey God's message, must have made a considerable impression, and is an indispensable item in any consideration of the performance side of the prophetic ministries.

By concentrating in this lecture on the performance side of the work of the prophets I have neglected the poetic side, and this I must put right in next week's lecture. I shall consider the four so-called Servant Songs in Isaiah 42-53 as poetry, and ask what such an approach can tell us about what they mean.

The Servant Songs of Isaiah 42-53

If Robert Lowth changed the way we read the Bible, Bernhard Duhm changed the way we read Isaiah 40-66. In his commentary published in 1892, Duhm made two suggestions that have claimed the attention of all subsequent commentators, whether they agree with his suggestions or not. The first was that chapters 56-66 came from a later date and a different prophetic tradition compared with chapters 40-55. The second suggestion was that there was a set of poems, particularly in chapters 40-55, that describe a Servant of God who differs in significant ways from Israel, the servant of God, in other parts of the book.[51]

The suggestion concerning the Servant Songs, as they have come to be called, has generated an enormous amount of

---

[51] B. Duhm, *Das Buch Jesaia*, (1892), 5th ed., Göttingen: Vandenhoeck & Ruprecht, 1968. In fact, almost a hundred years before Duhm, E. F. K. Rosenmüller had suggested in his *Scholia in Vetus Testamentum*, pt. 3, Jesajae vaticinia complectentis sect. 2, Leipzig, 1793, that the four pieces belonged together and dealt with the prophet and his office. However, it was Duhm's commentary which affected subsequent scholarship. An original approach to the subject by a scholar who did not accept Duhm's conclusions can be found in J. D. Smart, *History and Theology in Second Isaiah. A Commentary on Isaiah 35, 40-66*, London: Epworth Press, 1967.

literature. Were the Songs written by the same person who wrote the rest of chapters 40-55 or are they by a different prophet? How did they come to be inserted into chapters 40-55, and was this done haphazardly, or according to a plan? Even more controversy has been generated by attempts to identify the Servant. For traditional Christian interpretation, the Servant material was a prophecy of the ministry of Jesus, a conclusion secured by the fact that the first Song, Isaiah 42.1-5 is quoted in full in Matthew 12.18-21. When critical scholarship began to try to understand the Songs in the context of the time of composition of chapters 40-55, there was, and remains, little agreement. Is the Servant an individual and, if so, who is he? Or is the Servant a corporate figure, such as an ideal Israel, or a prophetic group within Israel? It is not my intention to engage with these questions. Although they are important, too much attention has been paid to them, to the detriment of trying to read the Songs as poetry, and this is what I shall attempt to do this evening.

Here is the first Song, Isaiah 42.1-5, in my translation:

> Here is my Servant, whom I have embraced,
> My chosen one in whom I delight.
> I have clothed him with my spirit;
> He will bring forth justice to the nations.
> He will not cry out or raise his voice,
> Nor make himself to be heard in the street.
> He will not snap a bent reed,
> Nor quench a flickering wick.
> He will surely bring forth justice.
> He will not tire nor be diverted
> Until he has established justice on the earth,
> And the Islands long for his teaching.

If you cast your minds back to last week's lecture and the messenger formula, you will remember that it assumed that the prophet had stood in the very presence of God and had heard God deliver a message for a king or a people, which the prophet was to repeat verbatim to those for whom it was intended. In this first Song, the Servant is in God's presence, not in order to hear a message that he then has to deliver, but to be introduced by God to the hearers and readers of the Song as God's Servant. The affirmation of the Servant could not be stronger. God has embraced him, has endued him with the spirit of wisdom, understanding and the fear of God, and has entrusted him with a universal mission, that of establishing justice and order among the nations.

We are now faced with a paradox. This Servant is not to be a performer like the prophets we studied last week. He is not to cry out in the streets or otherwise raise his voice. How, then, can he undertake his mission? To these two negatives, two other negatives are added. He will not snap a bent reed, nor quench a flickering wick. What does this mean? The commentators try to link these words with possible modes of action; but we must not be tempted to do this. As we saw two weeks ago, sometimes the only way that something significant can be said is by way of negatives. If the poem had wanted to specify particular practical courses of action, it could have done so. To use negatives is to say in effect that what is envisaged cannot be adequately stated. We must leave the matter there and hope for enlightenment later. Whatever will be the method or methods of carrying out the divine task, the Servant will not tire or be diverted from his work until it has been accomplished. He will be pushing at open doors. The coastlands and Islands wait in longing to hear his message.

The second Song is found in Isaiah 49.1-6:

> Pay attention to me, you islands

And listen, you peoples from afar.
The LORD called me from the womb,
And named me in my mother's loins.
He made my mouth a sharp sword
And hid me in the shadow of his hand.
He made me like a burnished arrow
And concealed me in his quiver.
He said, 'You are my Servant, Israel,
The one through whom I shall get glory'.
But I said, 'I have toiled for nothing,
I have wasted my strength for chaos and vanity'.
Even so, my vindication will come from the LORD,
And my reward from my God.

But now speaks the LORD who formed me in the womb to
be his Servant
To being back Jacob to him
And to gather Israel to him,
(And I am honoured in the LORD's eyes
And my God has become my strength),
He says
To be my Servant to restore the tribes of Jacob
And to bring back the lost ones of Israel
is too light a thing.
I shall make you a light to the nations
That my salvation may reach to the ends of the earth.

The second Song begins where the first one left off, with a reference to the Islands who are waiting eagerly for God's teaching. But something seems to have gone wrong. The Servant addresses the Islands, but seems to have to justify his mission to them by rehearsing the credentials he received from God. Does this mean that the message was not received on its own account, so that it needed to be justified by appeal to God's endorsement of the Servant? Was it the message or the messenger that was the problem? Was the message that the Islands heard a different one from what they expected or wanted to hear?

The Servant appears to have lost heart, and to regard his labours as fruitless. When he says, 'I have wasted my strength for chaos and vanity', the words that I have translated as 'chaos' and 'vanity' are significant. The 'chaos' word *tohu* comes in Genesis 1, when the earth is described as waste and void, before God establishes order. The word rendered 'vanity', *hevel*, occurs in Ecclesiastes 1, where the writer regards his many achievements as ultimately vanity and a striving after wind. The Servant is saying that the result of his labours is to leave untouched a world that is chaotic, that lacks God's order, a world whose values amount to nothing lasting. In this situation of despair the Servant finds his only consolation in God.

But God speaks to repeat his confidence in the Servant. This confidence is reinforced by a reminder that a mission to the Servant's own people is an easy one. God has a greater purpose, and that is for his salvation to be known to the ends of the earth; paradoxically, this task is to be carried out by a Servant who believes that he has failed, and toiled for nothing.

Before I move on to the third Song I must refer briefly to the occurrence of the name Israel in the second Song. It has generated much discussion, because it seems to settle once and for all the question of whether the Servant is an individual or a corporate figure. In fact, those who take the view that the Servant is an individual whom they try to identify have not been deterred by the reference to Israel. There have even been attempts to argue that 'Israel' is a later addition to the text. I do not intend to enter the discussion, but merely point out that my translation assumes that the words should be taken together as 'You are my Servant, Israel; the one through whom I shall get glory', as against the alternative, 'You are my servant; Israel through whom I shall get glory.'

The third Song appears in 50.4-9:

> The Lord GOD has given me the tongue of a disciple,
> That I may know to help the weary with a word that
> revives.
> Morning by morning he awakens my ear
> To hear as those who are instructed.
> The Lord GOD has awakened my ear,
> And I have neither rebelled, nor turned away.
> My back I have given to the smiters
> And my cheeks to those who pulled out my beard.
> I have not hidden my face from reproach or spitting.
> Surely the Lord GOD is my helper,
> Therefore have I not been put to shame.
> I have set my fact like flint,
> And know that I shall not be ashamed.
> He who fights my cause is close,
> Who will contend with me?
> Let us stand together.
> Who disputes my cause?
> Let him come against me!
> It is the Lord GOD who helps me,
> Who will put me in the wrong?
> They will surely wear out like a garment;
> The moth will devour them.

The language of the third Song suggests the law court and legal proceedings as its background. This is indicated by the verbs that I have translated as 'fights my cause', 'contend', 'disputes' and 'put me in the wrong'. These all have to do with accusing, condemning, defending and acquitting people in a legal context. The language about punishment also points in this direction. Flogging is mentioned as a penalty in Deuteronomy 25.2, while Nehemiah 13.25 speaks of pulling out the hair of those who are punished by Nehemiah. Spitting in the face is mentioned several times (Numbers 12.14, Deuteronomy 25.9) as a way of shaming those against whom accusations have been brought. It is clear that the Servant has suffered these humiliations unjustly. The poem implies that they resulted from the fact that he had listened most profoundly to what God had to say. His was not an occasional appearance in God's presence in the divine court to hear so as to deliver a message. The Servant was taught morning by morning and stuck faithfully to the instructions he was given. The poem raises the unanswerable question about what can be done when someone is prosecuted, condemned and punished for speaking a truth that is believed to come from God. At one level, we may say, cynically, that there have been too many people in human history who were convinced that they were right and that everyone else was wrong; too many people who believed that they, alone, had access to God's will and words. However, for most, if not all, of such people the invocation of the authority of God was designed to give themselves power over other people. Power over other people is the last thing that is experienced by the Servant in the servant poems; and the defence of justice at the cost of a person's popularity or safety is something that is found in other prophetic books, as well as in the Psalms.

Amos condemns those who want to turn justice into wormwood (a bitter plant, *artemisia herba-alba*)[52] and want to undermine righteousness (Amos 5.7). He further condemns those who abhor the speaking of truth and the proper administration of justice before the elders who meet in the city gate (Amos 5.10). Micah condemns those who build Sion with blood and Jerusalem with wrong, and elaborates this by saying that its rulers administer justice on the basis of bribery (Micah 3.9-10). The most scathing language on this subject comes in Psalm 94, when the question is asked,

---

[52] M. Zohari, *Plants of the Bible*, Cambridge: Cambridge University Press, 1982, p. 184.

Can those who cover up their wickedness have you [God]
as an ally,
Those who produce evil by passing laws?
They band themselves against the life of the righteous
And condemn the innocent to death (vv.20-21).[53]

The third Song's importance is the way in which it describes
the intimate relationship that exists between the Servant and
God: in the daily waiting upon God's instruction, and in the
confident assertion that God is the Servant's helper and that
he will not be put (ultimately) to shame. There are echoes in
these latter words of Paul's declaration in Romans 8 that
nothing can separate from the love of God those for whom
God has given his Son. We are not, then, dealing with
someone who is merely distressed in a general way with the
practical denials of truth and justice that marred the ancient
world as they also mar today's world. The Servant's
relationship with God is such that the denial of justice is a
denial of God. It is as though we were caught up in a situation
in which someone to whom we were very close was being
falsely accused of wrongdoing. We would be affronted not
only by the wrongness on the case. We would feel for the
person being wronged in a way that would affect our feelings
also. Their vindication would not only bring us satisfaction
that right had prevailed. It would bring us joy that someone
about whom we cared had been put into the right. With these
thoughts, we turn to the fourth and longest Song, in Isaiah
52.13-53.12:

Behold, my Servant will succeed,
And be lifted, exalted and very high.
For just as many were offended at him,
(his appearance was so marred that he scarcely seemed
human)

---

[53] Translation in J. W. Rogerson, *The Psalms in Daily Life*, London: SPCK, 2001, p.38. See the whole section entitled 'Psalms crying out for Justice'.

Yet shall he amaze many nations.
Kings shall be silenced because of him,
for they shall see things they had not been told,
and understand what they had not heard.
Who could have believed what we have heard?
To whom could the arm of the LORD have been revealed?
He grew up like an ugly plant
Like a root out of dry ground.
He had no fine appearance or majestic looks
That might attract us to him,
He was despised and rejected,
A man bowed down by sorrows
and burdened with pain,
As one from whom men instinctively turn away,
We also despised and took no account of him.
Yet somehow he has borne our infirmities
And carried our afflictions,
Although we believed that it was by God
That he was struck, beaten and humiliated.
But he was wounded because of our rebelling,
Crushed because of our wrong-doing,
Upon him came the punishment that was our restoration,
And his beatings brought us healing.
We have all of us erred like sheep,
Turned each one to his own ways,
And the LORD has made the guilt of all of us
rest upon him.
He was oppressed and humiliated
Yet opened not his mouth.
Like a sheep brought to the slaughter house
And a ewe before its shearers
He kept silence, and opened not his mouth.
Unjustly and violently he was taken away,
And who noticed where he was being taken?[54]
He was cut off from the land of the living
Punished for the sin of his people.[55]
His burial place was among the wicked,
His resting-place with workers of evil[56]

---

[54] Reading *darko* for *doro.*
[55] Reading *'ammo.*
[56] Reading *'ose ra'* for *'ashir.*

73

Even though he had done no violence,
Nor had he spoken deceit.
Yet the LORD was pleased with his pain,
Making atonement with his life.[57]
He will see offspring and long life,
And the LORD's pleasure will prosper at his hand.
Through the toil of his life he will see light, and be
satisfied.
By his knowledge will my Servant justify many
and bear their guilt.
Therefore I will give him a portion with the mighty
And with the powerful will he divide the spoil,
Because he gave up his life to death
And was numbered with transgressors.
He bore the sin of many
And entreated for their offences.

The fourth of the Servant Songs is one of the most difficult Hebrew passages in the Bible to translate and understand. It has generated more scholarly literature than any other passage, and it would be wrong if I were to create the impression that in a few minutes I can solve all its problems and say something definitive about it. I hope merely to make some comments that will be appropriate to the theme of these lectures, the prophets as poets.

Like the first Song, the fourth Song begins with God speaking about his servant. This time, he does not introduce the Servant, but speaks about the paradoxical success that he is going to achieve, a success that will confound all outward impressions. The song moves to speakers who speak in the first person plural. Who are they? Are they the kings who are mentioned in the first part of the poem? We do not know, but as the song continues, interpreters find themselves under the

---

[57] See H-J. Hermisson, *Deuterojesaja*, Biblischer Kommentar Altes Testament, XI, 16, Neukirchen: Neukirchener Verlag, 2012, p. 329, who describes this as the hardest verse in the whole passage to translate and understand.

greatest pressure to see the Servant as an individual and to identify him and the things that are said about him. The text says that he grew up like an ugly plant and like a root out of dry ground. Does this mean that he was born disabled, or that he had contracted a disfiguring disease, or did the marks that disfigured his appearance come from what he had suffered in imprisonment and punishment? What is clear is that the Servant is not a glamorous celebrity to whom people would be naturally attracted.

The next set of lines have, as their background, the law court and perhaps the imagery of the Day of Atonement. The language about the Servant being struck, beaten and humiliated, and about his punishment, suggest that the law court and the Servant are being unjustly accused, condemned and imprisoned. How these things could lead to the restoration and healing of those speaking in the first person plural can perhaps be understood in the context of the ritual of the Day of Atonement, where a goat was led into the wilderness bearing the sins which the congregation had confessed. That may be the background, but the thought is much more profound. This is not a matter of transferring guilt from one group to another person. It is much more that something has happened to the Servant which has struck the consciences and hearts of those who observed it or heard about it, so that they have reached the conclusion that what the Servant had suffered had been done for them personally. This realisation had brought them to a new awareness of themselves and their situation, which made them feel that they had been healed and restored.

The poem then moves on to speak about the death of the Servant. The theme of the Servant being punished on behalf of others is still present. His innocence is now fully recognized.

He had done no violence, and had spoken no deceit. It is then asserted that what he suffered was either God's plan, or acceptable to God. This verse is extremely difficult to translate and understand. What this assertion is doing is overturning the common belief in the Old Testament that misfortune and sickness are a sign of God's displeasure. The fourth Song turns this idea on its head. The unattractive appearance of the Servant, his trials and afflictions, his unjust conviction and punishment, had somehow been part of something deeper, through which suffering on behalf of others could bring life and hope to these others. Because of this, the Servant is to be rewarded. Although dead and buried, he will see offspring and have the satisfaction of knowing that his actions were not in vain; that those who had rejected and despised him will see his work in quite a different light. In the ultimate scheme of reality, he will be seen to be great, although in his life he was seen to be nothing and was rejected. Perhaps his life and suffering will help to define or redefine the meaning of 'greatness'.

Looking at the poems as a whole I want to suggest that there is an inside and an outside, and the question of how it is possible to get from the outside to the inside. I begin with the inside.

The inside is most clearly seen from the Servant's point of view in the second and third poems. The Servant states that he was called by God before he was born, and that he was named in his mother's womb. One thinks immediately here of the beginning of the Book of Jeremiah, where the prophet is told that he was called to be a prophet before he was born. This is no doubt a realisation that comes gradually to the prophet, and it must not be thought to be good news from an earthly perspective. We are not dealing with a life that is to be born to wealth and privilege, a life in which success will be assured by knowing the right people and moving in the best circles. To be called by God is to be called into danger, to be called into a dimension that puzzles and excites the hostility of the world that does not know or care about God. This dimension is described in the poems in language expressing hiddenness and intimacy. The prophet is like an arrow hidden in a quiver; each morning he listens to God's voice and is instructed in his task. Although he experiences despair at his apparent failures, he is enabled by God to persist in his work and to bear with fortitude the rejection and punishment that his work brings upon him.

The 'inside' is also described from God's point of view at the beginning of the first Song when God introduces the Servant. The Servant is clothed with God's spirit, and there is also a warning in this introduction that the Servant's task will confound human expectations. He will not speak aloud or draw attention to himself; he will not snap a bent rod or quench a flickering wick. At the beginning of the fourth Song God speaks of the assured success of the Servant in a poem that will speak of the Servant's physical ugliness and his humiliation at the hands of his fellow men. The 'inside' is known only to God as he calls the Servant to his service, and to the Servant as he carries out his task in close communion with God.

The 'outside' is represented by those who are offended at the Servant's appearance, who accuse, condemn and punish him, and who think that his misfortunes are a sign of God's displeasure. If I may return to the philosophy of knowledge which I invoked in the second lecture, the 'outsiders' can be likened to empirical thinking which draws conclusions on the basis of evidence presented to it. I am not, of course, implying that there is anything wrong with empirical thinking. We all need and use it all the time to navigate the world in which we live. But empirical thinking is only one kind of thinking, and it cannot embrace or understand the whole of reality. The liminal experiences of suffering and death expose the limitations of empirical thinking, and it is in poetic thought that these liminal things are addressed and wrestled with, or, to put it in terms of what I am saying in this lecture, it is poetic thought that is the 'inside' to the 'outside' of empirical thought. In the fourth Song, it is the suffering of the Servant that enables those on the outside, those who rejected him, to pass to the inside, to see the matter from the perspective of the Servant and of God. We might say that whoever or whatever the Servant is, he is the supreme poetic symbol in the Old Testament for that exploration of suffering in the service of God that enables people to see reality not only in an empirical sense, from the outside, but in a poetic sense, from the inside, and ultimately, in a divine sense.

If I am correct in saying this, that the Servant is the supreme poetic symbol in the Old Testament for the exploration of suffering that enables people to pass from the outside to the inside, it is no surprise that the Servant poems resonate so much with other parts of the Old Testament that are concerned with the outside and the inside of human experience. In the Book of Job, the three, and later four, comforters typify the outside. Job's misfortunes must be a deserved punishment for wrongs that he has committed. Job disagrees, and although he does not claim to be faultless, he maintains that there is no reason why God should want to punish him so disproportionately. He maintains his belief in God's justice, and at the end of the book we are told that God's wrath is kindled against the comforters because they had not spoken what was right. Their thought, as we would put it, had remained on the outside. It is noteworthy that in the Book of Job the comforters only speak *about* God, never *to* him. Job, on the other hand, speaks to God, sometimes arguing with him and accusing him of being unjust; but he has a relationship with God. Job is on the inside.

Another figure in the Old Testament that should be mentioned here is the prophet Jeremiah; and indeed, it has often been argued that the Servant of the Servant Songs should be identified with Jeremiah. His life is threatened because of his prophesying, he is accused of being a traitor, and he suffers the traumatic experience of being imprisoned in a cistern which, although it is dry, has mud at the bottom (Jeremiah 38.6) and no doubt the human excrement of others imprisoned there. At the end of his life, ordinary people accuse him of having brought upon them the miseries of conquest and exile that they are experiencing because they took notice of him and gave up the old popular superstitions that had sustained them before Jeremiah came on to the scene. Jeremiah sees the inside; that God is prepared to let Jerusalem be destroyed so that a new beginning can be made. The rulers and the people, not surprisingly, see the outside, the need for the city to withstand siege and destruction.

Another figure to be mentioned is Moses who, at Numbers 12.3 is described as being very meek, more than any other man. The Hebrew word *'naw* is hard to translate and probably hovers in meaning between shyness and modesty. Certainly, in Numbers 12, members of his own family dispute his right to lead them and to speak in God's name. Moses is constantly complained about by the people he has led from slavery to freedom. They represent the outside as they complain about the harsh conditions of the wilderness to which, they say, slavery was preferable.

It is no surprise that Christians reading the Servant Songs have seen them as foretellings of the sufferings and death of Jesus; and throughout the Gospels the theme of outside and inside is strongly represented. Neither the family, nor the disciples, nor the opponents of Jesus can understand who he is or what his mission is. They are on the outside. The paradox of his redeeming death, its outside and inside, is brilliantly summed up by St Paul when he says that the proclamation of Christ crucified is a stumbling block to the Jews and folly to the Greeks, but to those who are called, whether Jew or Greek, it is the power of God and the wisdom of God (1 Corinthians 1.23-4). Paul's realisation that Jesus was 'the Son of God who loved me and gave himself for me' (Galatians 2.20) enabled him to pass from the outside of persecuting the Church, to the inside of being its greatest missionary – and also one who suffered greatly for it.

So the Servant poems can be read as creating a link between an outside that corresponds to empirical thinking and an inside which corresponds to poetic thinking, with the suffering that an innocent person undergoes on behalf of others being a way in which people can pass from an outside of thinking that it is a tragedy or punishment to an inside of seeing it as redemptive. There is, of course, much suffering in the world that seems to be quite pointless, and I am not going to suggest that it has any meaning or that it is any way good. But not all suffering is meaningless. The message of the Servant Songs, read as poetry, is that it may be a means of hope and restoration.

There is one final question to be asked, which takes us on to next week. Do the sufferings which God's servants undergo for his sake also affect God? Do they leave him unmoved? This will be one of the questions to be considered when we ask next week what the poet prophets of the Old Testament may have to say to today's world.

LECTURE 5

What do the Prophet Poets of the Old Testament have to say to us today?

'Reading the Old Testament is like eating a large crab. It is mostly shell, with very little meat in it.' I have forgotten where I came upon this verdict on the Old Testament, but it was from, I think, a young Japanese Christian and I have been unable to track it down. I do remember, however, that it was followed by a quotation from the great German theologian Adolf von Harnack's book on Marcion, and this I was able to find elsewhere. Marcion, who was born around AD 85 in Sinope on the Black Sea, today just inside Turkey, founded a church that rejected the Old Testament entirely and had as its New Testament an edited version of Luke's Gospel and several of the letters of Paul. Marcion believed that the God of the Old Testament was a different God from that of Jesus and Paul. Harnack's observation went as follows (in my translation):

> To reject the Old Testament in the second century was a mistake that the great church rightly avoided. To retain it

in the sixteenth century was an outcome that the Reformation could not avoid. To retain it still since the nineteenth century in Protestantism as a canonical document was the result of religious and ecclesiastical paralysis.[58]

These two verdicts on the uselessness of the Old Testament could be matched by popular opinions today, both within and outside the churches. One hears it said that the God of the Old Testament is a God of hate and anger, that the Old Testament contains texts about genocide, rape and adultery, not to mention laws that can be summed up in the formula 'an eye for an eye'. People who make these comments have not usually read the Old Testament or, at best, have only read a tiny portion of it. Last week's lecture sought to explore the profound insights into the power of redemptive suffering in the Servant Songs of Isaiah 42-53. Today I want to explore the question of whether it is possible for God to suffer, and how the results of this exploration in the Old Testament prophets have much to say to the Church and the world today. The question arises out of last week's lecture. Does the fact that God calls people to suffer in his service mean that he is involved in that suffering or does he remain detached from it?

I begin by considering the work of a Jewish scholar, Abraham Joshua Heschel, who was born in Warsaw in 1907 into a family of distinguished Rabbis.[59] Heschel went to the

---

[58] A. von Harnack, *Marcion. Das Evangelium vom fremden Gott, Eine Monographie zur Geschichte der Grundlegung der katholischen Kirche*, 2nd ed. 1924, reprinted Darmstadt: Wissenschaftliche Buchgesellschaft, 1996, p. 217. 'Das AT im 2. Jahrhundert zu verwerfen, war ein Fehler, den die grosse Kirche mit Recht abgelehnt hat; es im 16. Jahrhundert beizuhalten, war ein Schicksal, dem sich die Reformation noch nicht zu entziehen vermochte; es aber seit dem 19.Jahrhundert als kanonische Urkunde im Protestantlismus noch zu Konservieren, ist die Folge einer religiösen und kirchlichen Lähmung'.

[59] E. J. Kaplan, S. H. Dresner, *Abraham Joshua Heschel. Prophetic Witness*, New Haven: Yale University Press, 1998.

University of Berlin in 1927 to study for a doctorate in the philosophical faculty. He was influenced by the Jewish German philosophers active in Germany, such as Martin Buber, Hermann Cohen and Ernst Cassirer. In 1932/33 he completed a dissertation on the subject of the prophetic consciousness, and was awarded the degree in 1936, having experienced great difficulty in fulfilling one of the requirements for the award of the doctorate, that of getting the dissertation published. Measures against Jews were already beginning to bite following Hitler's rise to power in 1933.

The traditional Christian view of how the prophets were inspired by God was that the prophets were passive receivers and writers of words that God dictated to them through the Holy Spirit. Mediaeval art often depicts biblical writers sitting or standing at a writing desk with the Holy Spirit in the form of a bird perched near their right ear, communicating God's words. A Jewish view was that the prophets received communications from God through visionary experiences.

With the rise of critical scholarship, the prophets were rescued from the role of being merely passive writers to that of being active preachers, addressing their hearers concerning the present and the future. This raised the question of how they were inspired by God; how God communicated his will to them. There are in fact some interesting hints in the prophetic books themselves that suggest that prophets sometimes saw ordinary things that suggested God's word to them. Jeremiah sees an almond tree, in Hebrew a *shaqed,* and receives or feels the divine word that God is looking after (*shokqed*) his word to fulfil it (Jeremiah 1.11-12). Jeremiah also sees a pot set to the north boiling over, and proclaims that a foe will come upon Jerusalem from the north (Jeremiah 1.13). Amos sees a basket of summer fruits (Hebrew *qaits*) and is told that the end (*qets*) has come upon God's people (Amos 8.2). These hints are most helpful; yet they do not explain how the prophets came to formulate their poetry in the way that they did.

Prior to Heschel, some scholars had been investigating prophetic inspiration in the light of psychological theories of the early twentieth century, laying stress upon paranormal ecstatic experiences. This was the challenge that Heschel faced, and in dealing with it he put forward a theory of what he called 'divine pathos', which has generated much discussion. I first came across Heschel in my Durham days while supervising a research student, and I still possess the extensive notes that I took while reading Heschel's dissertation in the university library in Tübingen over forty years ago.[60]

Heschel's immediate predecessors had investigated the psychology of the prophets. For Heschel, prophecy resulted from what he called a theophany, a movement from God towards the prophets in which an encounter took place. Heschel's task was not to investigate the psychology of the prophets, but to describe and seek to understand the nature of the divine-human meeting that resulted in prophecy. Heschel used the analogy of two people meeting.[61] When A meets B and describes B as a result of this meeting, what he describes is not the essence and being of the person met, but how the meeting registered itself on A. Similarly, the encounter between the prophets and God was an event which registered on the prophets. They tried to describe what it was that they had experienced, but necessarily had to do it in their own language. What they experienced in general was described by

---

[60] Heschel published a revised version of his dissertation in English. See A. J. Heschel, *The Prophets*, 2 vols., New York: Harper & Row, 1969, 1975.

[61] A. J. Heschel, *Das prophetische Bewusstsein*, Diss. Berlin 1936, p. 101.

Heschel as 'divine pathos', a term that was deliberately vague or opaque and needing to be filled with meaning with the help of various examples. Pathos was *not* a projection of human feelings on to God; it described not God's being, but what happened in the encounter between God and the prophet. It was a relational term.[62] The response of the prophets was called by Heschel *Sympathie,* by which he meant a response that captured authentically what the divine initiatives had intended, while at the same time the language used by the prophets was not to be taken literally as describing God. The task of interpreting the writings of the prophets involved finding a way of saying what the prophets had experienced in their encounter with God, the encounter with his pathos, without taking their language literally, as though in some way it described the being and essence of God. This is an important point that requires elaboration.

Jewish tradition has set its face immovably against the idea that God has any passions or feelings. The opening part of the great Arabic work by the Jewish philosopher Maimonides, the *Dalālat alHaireen* (*The Guide of the Perplexed*) of 1190 argues remorselessly that language about God's bodily parts and emotions must not be taken literally.[63] God does not see, or speak, or know, or have a hand, or an eye, or an ear. Biblical language that says that God does do and have these things must not be taken literally. The issue is the avoidance of anthropomorphism, of representing God in human terms. If God is represented in this way, he becomes a human creation,

---

[62] Heschel, *Bewusstsein*, p. 146. Pathos 'bedeutet kein Sosein, sondern ein Sobezogensein.'

[63] M. Maimonides, *Dalālat alHaireen*, Arabic text with Hebrew translation by J. Qapha, Jerusalem: Mossad Harav Kook, 1972; English translation by S. Pines, Chicago: University of Chicago Press, 1963.

an idol; and the prophetic condemnation of idolatry is devastating:

> Their idols are like scarecrows in a cucumber field,
> They cannot speak,
> They have to be carried
> for they cannot walk.
> Be not afraid of them,
> They cannot do evil,
> Neither is it in them to do good. (Jeremiah 10.5)

Idols are human creations and as such have no power to help or save.

The Christian view on these things is clearly stated in the first of the 39 Articles of Religion of the Church of England:

> There is but one living and true God, everlasting, without body, parts, or passions.

Heschel does a helpful job in interpreting the language used by the prophets, so that they can be seen to express what humans would call emotions, without compromising the fact that any human language about God is inadequate, and totally misleading if taken literally. He interprets language about the anger or wrath of God as expressions of a divine involvement in human affairs that is born of a concern for justice and goodness. It is, writes Heschel, 'der tatsächliche Erweis der Liebe Gottes'.[64] This matter has, of course, relevance for the point made at the beginning of this lecture, namely, the objection brought against the Old Testament that it portrays a God of anger and vengeance. This objection is only valid if such language is to be taken literally. Jewish and Christian tradition says that it should not be taken literally.

---

[64] Heschel, *Bewusstsein*, p. 150.

Is this special pleading by Jewish and Christian tradition, an attempt to justify the unjustifiable? Can the charge be brought that while it may be comforting for us to feel that God suffers emotions of love and compassion, we feel uncomfortable with the idea of God being angry and wrathful, and need to find ways of explaining this away? A criticism has been brought against Heschel from within the Jewish philosophical community, which has accused him of coming too close to saying that God suffers, a notion alien to Judaism.[65] This dispute is not one on which a Christian should comment, but it is one from which Christians can learn much. In answer to the question, 'Does God suffer?' I would say that we must not project our ideas and feelings of suffering on to God, but accept that biblical language about God suffering describes something real.

For the moment, I want to turn from theory to practice, and to translate and comment on a passage in Isaiah 55.1-11 that has much to say to this whole matter: [66]

> Listen! All who are thirsty, come to the waters,
> Whoever has no money, come!
> Buy and eat, without money[67]
> and without price, wine and milk.
> Why do you weigh out your silver
> For what is not bread,
> And toil for what does not satisfy?
> Listen indeed to me and eat what is good,
> Let your souls feast on fatness.

---

[65] See essay, 'The practical proof of the love of God', by E. Berkovits, in *Major Themes in Modern Philosophies of Judaism*, New York: Ktav, 1974, pp. 192-224.
[66] For an exhaustive commentary on this passage see H.-J. Hermisson, *Deuterojesaja*, Biblischer Kommentar Altes Testament, XI, 19-20, Neukirchen: Neukirchener Verlag, 2016, pp. 572-654.
[67] Omitting *ulekhu shivru* as a dittograph.

Bend your ears and come to me,
Listen and let your souls live,
And I will make an everlasting covenant with you,
The true mercies shown to David.
I made him a witness to the nations,
A ruler and instructor to peoples.
Indeed, you will call to a nation you do not know,
And a nation that knows you not will run to you,
Because of the LORD your God
And the Holy One of Israel,
because he has glorified you.

Seek the LORD, for he can be found,
Call upon him, because he is near.
Let the wicked forsake his ways
And the evildoer his thoughts,
And return to the LORD, for he will have mercy on him,
And to our God, for he will richly forgive him.
Surely, my thoughts are not your thoughts,
And my ways are not your ways, says the LORD.
The heavens are high over the earth,
And so are my ways higher than your ways,
And my thoughts higher than your thoughts.
As the rain comes down,
And the snow from heaven,
And returns not thence
Until it has watered the earth,
And has made it bring forth life and growth,
Giving seed to the sower
And bread to the eater,
So shall my word be that goes forth from my mouth.
It will not return to me empty
Until it has done what pleases me,
And successfully accomplished that for which I sent it.

This passage illustrates some of the points that I have been making in these lectures. Thinking back to the first lecture, the passage is replete with parallelism:

Seek the LORD, for he can be found,
Call upon him, because he is near.

Let the wicked forsake his ways
And the evildoer his thoughts,
And return to the LORD, for he will have mercy on him,
And to our God, for he will richly forgive him.
Surely, my thoughts are not your thoughts,
And my ways are not your ways, says the LORD.
The heavens are high over the earth,
And so are my ways higher than your ways,
And my thoughts higher than your thoughts.

The passage also begins with a performance, something emphasised in the third lecture. The prophet appears in the role of a salesman, a salesman who is offering bargains that are bound to attract an audience:

Listen! All who are thirsty, come to the waters,
Whoever has no money, come!
Buy and eat, without money[68]
and without price, wine and milk.

I am reminded of a shopkeeper in the old city of Jerusalem who was offering one hundred per cent discounts! However, having attracted an audience, the prophet speaks in God's name of the futility of lives devoted purely and simply to material things, when there are life-giving words from God:

Why do you weigh out your silver
For what is not bread,
And toil for what does not satisfy?
Listen indeed to me and eat what is good,
Let your souls feast on fatness.
Bend your ears and come to me,
Listen and let your souls live,

The passage also connects with Heschel's attempts to account for prophetic inspiration, and indeed the following lines are quoted by Heschel to make the point that whatever may be

---

[68] Omitting *ulekhu shivru* as a dittograph.

said about the moment of prophetic contact with God and the resulting human language, there is an unbridgeable gulf between the human and the divine, a gulf that can only be bridged from God's side as and when God in his freedom wills this: [69]

> Surely, my thoughts are not your thoughts,
> And my ways are not your ways, says the LORD.
> The heavens are high over the earth,
> And so are my ways higher than your ways,
> And my thoughts higher than your thoughts.

And yet the prophet urges his hearers to seek God, because he can be found. The traditional rendering of these verses in the Authorized Version and translations in its tradition is 'Seek ye the LORD while he may be found'. The difficulty with this rendering is that it may convey the impression that what is on offer has a sell-by date, after which a special offer will be withdrawn; and I have heard the text used in this way at missions by preachers who wanted hearers to reach a decision before the mission ended. The Hebrew literally means, 'Seek the LORD in his being found' or to put it in other words, 'given that he can be found', which is why I have rendered it 'because he can be found'. If there is any implied limit in the words, it is not a time limit but a limit of manner; God can be found only in the way that he chooses to be found, although the initiative comes from him, especially in the message of the prophets.

The words that immediately precede the magnificent assertion that God's ways and thoughts are beyond the comprehension of human understanding point up sharply the dilemma that Heschel was addressing. The prophet asserts that God will

---

[69] Heschel, *The Prophets*, vol. 1, p. 148.

have mercy on the repentant sinner and richly forgive him. The language about having mercy and forgiving, taken literally, can lure us into anthropomorphism, into ascribing to God the human characteristics that we associate with having mercy and forgiving. In order to avoid this, at any rate when speaking theologically, we must look for words that express the reality while avoiding the anthropomorphism. We might say that the wrongdoing that separates us from God, both objectively and in our feelings about our relationship with him, is dealt with from God's side, so that it loses the power to mar our relationship with God and opens up a future that we can face with the confidence that, in a mysterious but nevertheless real way, God is with us and for us.

The final verses of the passage, which liken the operation of God's words spoken by the prophets to the mysterious processes that operate in nature, whereby food and flowers spring from the earth when watered, are a magnificent reminder of how it is poetry above all else that enables mysteries to be expressed that lie beyond the powers of empirical thinking.

But I have said nothing about those verses in the passage that appear to forecast the future, to exhibit what has traditionally been thought to be the essence of prophecy:

> I will make an everlasting covenant with you,
> The true mercies shown to David.
> I made him a witness to the nations,
> A ruler and instructor to peoples.
> Indeed, you will call to a nation you do not know,
> And a nation that knows you not will run to you,
> Because of the LORD your God
> And the Holy One of Israel,
> because he has glorified you.

Christian interpretation has seen in this passage a prophecy of the mission of Christ. Matthew Poole, the Puritan commentator, sees David as a true type of Christ and the passage as an anticipation of his universal victory.[70] From the perspective of these lectures, which see the prophets primarily as poets seeing deeply into the present, a present that is eternally present, I would say that the passage speaks of the present rather than the future. If the hearers of the prophet respond and turn to God they will find true satisfaction, a satisfaction that will be here and now, and not at some future date, enabling then to enter the covenantal mercies shown by God to his people, and exemplified in God's promises to David. They will exhibit a covenant of grace that will attract other nations by the quality of the God-given mercies lived out in human lives. If the passage appears to be appropriate to the future, this is because in God, and in poetry, time does not work backwards and forwards, but in terms of an ever-present 'now'.

I return to Heschel, and as I said earlier, he has come in for a great deal of criticism from Jewish philosophers for not avoiding the dangers of anthropomorphism. It seems to me that he could have avoided this criticism by saying that the language of the prophets was the language of poetry. Perhaps he didn't say this, because to say that something is poetry is to give the impression that it does not belong to the real world, but that it belongs to a world of fiction; and Heschel certainly believed in the reality of God's initiative into human affairs. But in my second lecture I discussed the view of poetry found in the philosophy of knowledge of Gerd Wolandt, where it was asserted that poetry is a way of thinking, and pointed out that it is poetic thought and language, not empirical thought,

---

[70] Poole, *Commentary*, vol. 1, p. 453.

that is needed to cope with the liminal situations of death and suffering, not to mention experiences of the sublime and beautiful. To say that the language of the prophets is poetry, which it is, enables us to accept that what is said about God in anthropomorphic language is not to be taken literally, but poetically. The language is saying something real, but poetic language is indispensable if we are to speak meaningfully of God, whose thoughts are not our thoughts and whose ways are not our ways, yet who cares for his world, seeks those who will respond to him and calls some to his service, a service that may involve pain, suffering and death.

Like many poets, the prophets saw into the present in such a profound way that the present that they saw was an eternal present. This is one reason why what the prophets have to say about suffering, and their insights into human nature and the injustices and corruptions of human society, resonate profoundly down the ages. It is the reason why Jesus found in the prophetic traditions his unique way of understanding and expressing his mission of redemptive suffering. If this is correct, the Church desperately needs to reclaim the Old Testament in general and the prophets in particular.

There should be an end to the practice of having an Old Testament reading in a service which is prescribed not for its own sake, but because it is seen in some way to be a means to an end, the end being that of illustrating or connecting in some way to what is found in the New Testament readings. Further, we need to listen to what the Old Testament prophets are saying about God, particularly as we do that in the spirit of Jewish scholars such as Abraham Joshua Heschel. What was unique about the Old Testament prophets as poets was the fact that their poetry stemmed from an encounter with God, an encounter with God which necessarily required the language of poetry for it to be expressed. The prophets spoke in a realistic way about a God whose ways and thoughts were beyond human comprehension, but who wished to be sought and known in ways that could only be expressed poetically, in language resembling that of human emotions. The Church needs to take seriously the prophetic language about the incomparability and the unapproachability of God, except when and as he allows himself to be approached, and takes the initiative in doing so. There are many magnificent passages in the Old Testament prophets about the incomparability of God, and it would be well if churches thought deeply about these passages, especially where there is a temptation to represent God as nothing more than a kindly benevolent heavenly parent, whom we create in our own image, while taking offence at anything that suggests his judgement or anger. We need to remember that the judgement of God is part of the good news, the good news that a world marred so much by human wickedness and selfishness stands and will stand under the judgement of the God of righteousness and truth and peace.

There used to be a book entitled, *The Bible designed to be read as literature*. It may well be that there is a book entitled 'The Old Testament prophets designed to be read as poetry', but if there is not such a book, I would certainly like to see one, and for it to have wide circulation in the churches. Obviously, the passages would need to be carefully chosen and commented upon, so that they would help to make known, to the Church and to the world, the amazing witness of the prophet poets of the Old Testament to the reality of God and to the nature of the world in which we live.

I began these lectures by referring to the sermon I preached in May 2016 in Llansantffraed on 1 Samuel 3.1: 'The word of the

LORD was a rare in those days; there was no frequent vision (of prophecy)'. The situation described in this text is as true now as when 1 Samuel was written, and the aim of these lectures has been to elaborate the few words that I was able to say in the sermon. There is much more that could have been said, but I hope that I have covered the subject from points of view that will be informative and illuminating, and a basis for further work. In Old Testament scholarship, the burden of interpreting the prophets has, understandably, been carried out in the light of the concrete situations in which the prophets found themselves, and to which they spoke the word of God. While all that is important, I believe that much more attention needs to be paid to the poetic side of the Old Testament prophets, and to the implications of their poetic language for understanding God and for talking about God. Here, I think that Christians have much to learn from the Jewish tradition, and from scholars such as Abraham Joshua Heschel. It would, perhaps, be appropriate for me to end these lectures with a quotation from a prophet. It is a quotation that contains parallelism, it is a quotation that implies the incomparability of God, it is a quotation that implicitly criticises a world that seeks to exist without God and to be indifferent to his values. The words come from the Book of Jeremiah:

> Let not the wise man glory in his wisdom,
> Let not the mighty man glory in his might,
> Let not the rich man glory in his riches
> But let him who glories glory in this, that he understands
> and knows me,
> That I am the LORD who practise mercy, justice and
> righteousness in the earth;
> for in these things I delight, says the LORD.
> (Jeremiah 9.23-4, Hebrew 22-23) [71]

---

[71] Modern versions print out these verses as prose rather than poetry, but the poetic structure, evident in the Hebrew, is also clear in translation.

Bibliography

Ackroyd, P. R., Evans, C. F.

The Cambridge History of the Bible, Vol 1, From the Beginnings to Jerome, Cambridge: Cambridge University Press, 1970.

Barrett, C. K.

'The Interpretation of the Old Testament in the New' in P. R. Ackroyd, C. F. Evans, *The Cambridge History of the Bible, Vol. 1, From the Beginnings to Jerome,* Cambridge: Cambridge University Press, 1970, pp. 377-411.

Berkovits, E.

Major Themes in Modern Philosophies of Judaism, New York: Ktav, 1974.

Coleridge, S. T.

'Songs of the Pixies V' in H. J. Jackson (ed.), *Samuel Taylor Coleridge,* Oxford: Oxford University Press, 1985.

Duhm, B.

Das Buch Jesaia, (1892), 5th ed., Göttingen: Vandenhoeck & Ruprecht, 1968.

Fries, J. F.

Julius und Evagoras. Ein philosophischer Roman, Göttingen: Vandenhoeck & Ruprecht, 1910.

Gray, G. B.

The Forms of Hebrew Poetry considered with Special Reference to the Criticism and Interpretation of the Old Testament, London: Hodder and Stoughton, 1915.

Gregory, G. (trans.)

Lectures on the Sacred Poetry of the Hebrews, 2 vols, London: J. Johnson, 1787.

Gundolf, F.

George, Berlin: Georg Bondi, 1930, 3rd ed. of the 1920 book.

Hare, F.

Psalmorum liber, in versiculos metrice divisus, 1736.

Hermisson, H.-J.

Deuterojesaja, Biblischer Kommentar Altes Testament, XI, 16, Neukirchen: Neukirchener Verlag, 2012.

Hermisson, H.-J.

Deuterojesaja, Biblischer Kommentar Altes Testament, XI, 19-20, Neukirchen: Neukirchener Verlag, 2016.

Heschel, A. J.

Das prophetische Bewusstsein, Diss., Berlin, 1936.

Heschel, A. J.

The Prophets, 2 vols., New York: Harper & Row, 1969, 1975.

Jackson, H. J. (ed.)

Samuel Taylor Coleridge, Oxford: Oxford University Press, 1985.

Jarick, J. (ed.)

Sacred Conjectures. The Context and Legacy of Robert Lowth and Jean Astruc, New York: T. & T. Clark, 2007.

Jeremias, J.

Der Prophet Amos (Das Alte Testament Deutsch 24, 2), Göttingen: Vandenhoeck & Ruprecht, 1995.

Kaplan, E. J., Dresner, S. H.

Abraham Joshua Heschel. Prophetic Witness, New Haven: Yale University Press, 1998.

Kaufmann, Y.

Toldot HaEmunah HaYisraelit, Tel Aviv: Devir, 1964.

Kugel, J. L.

The Idea of Biblical Poetry. Parallelism and its History, New Haven and London: Yale University Press, 1981

Lang, B.

Monotheism and the Prophetic Minority (Social World of Biblical Antiquity Series, 1), Sheffield: Almond Press, 1983.

Lowth, R.

De sacra poesie Hebraeorum. Praelectiones Academicae, Oxford: Clarendon Press, 1810, 2 vols., with annotations by J. D. Michaelis, English translation by G. Gregory, *Lectures on the Sacred Poetry of the Hebrews,* 2 vols, London: J. Johnson, 1787, this edition includes the notes by Michaelis and others.

Lowth, R.

Isaiah. A New Translation with a Preliminary Dissertation and Notes, Glasgow: Longman and others, 1822.

Lowth, R.

Memoirs of the Life and Worship of the late Right Reverend Robert Lowth, London: W Best, 1787.

Maimonides, M.

Dalālat alHaireen, Arabic text, with Hebrew translation by J. Qapha, Jerusalem: Mossad Harav Kook, 1972; English translation by S. Pines, Chicago: University of Chicago Press, 1963.

Martinez, F. G., *et al.* (eds.)

The Scriptures and the Scrolls. Studies in Honour of A S van der Woude on the Occasion of his 65th Birthday, Leiden: E. J. Brill, 1992.

Müller, G.

'Schöttgen, Johann Christoph in *Allgemeine Deutsche Biographie*, 32 (1891), pp. 412-417.

Phillips, D. Z. (ed.)

Jakob Friedrich Fries, Dialogues on Morality and Religion, Oxford: Basil Blackwell, 1982.

Plato

Republic, Book 10.

Poole, M.

A Commentary on the Holy Bible (1700), Edinburgh: Banner of Truth, 1962.

Rogerson, J. W.

Cultural Landscapes and the Bible. Collected Essays, Sheffield: Beauchief Abbey Press, 2014.

Rogerson, J. W.

The Psalms in Daily Life, London: SPCK, 2001.

Rogerson, J. W.

'Writing the History of Israel in the Seventeenth and Eighteenth Centuries' in F. G. Martinez *et al.* (eds.), *The Scriptures and the Scrolls. Studies in Honour of A. S. van der Woude on the Occasion of his 65th Birthday*, Leiden: E. J. Brill, 1992, pp. 217-27, reprinted in J. W. Rogerson, *Cultural Landscapes and the Bible. Collected Essays,* Sheffield: Beauchief Abbey Press, 2014, pp. 303-315.

Rosenmüller, E. F. K.

Scholia in Vetus Testamentum, pt. 3, Jesajae vaticinia complectentis, sect. 2, Leipzig, 1793.

Smart, J. D.

History and Theology in Second Isaiah. A Commentary on Isaiah 35, 40-66, London: Epworth Press, 1967.

Smith, R.

Handel's Oratorio Librettos and Eighteenth Century Thought, Cambridge: Cambridge University Press, 1995.

Watson, W. G. E.

'The Study of Hebrew Poetry: Past –Present – Future' in J. Jarick (ed.), *Sacred Conjectures. The Context and Legacy of Robert Lowth and Jean Astruc,* New York: T. & T. Clark, 2007, pp. 124-54.

Westermann, C.

Basic Forms of Prophetic Speech, London: Lutterworth Press, 1967.

Wildberger, H.

Jesaja (Biblischer Kommentar Altes Testament x/i), Neukirchen-Vluyn: Neukirchene Verlag, 1972.

Wolandt, G.

Philosophie der Dichtung. Weltstellung und Gegen-ständlichkeit des poetischen Gedankens, Berlin: de Gruyter, 1965.

Zohari, M.

Plants of the Bible, Cambridge: Cambridge University Press, 1982.

Zohari, M.

'bᵉushim' in *Enzyklopedia Hamiqrait,* vol. 2, Jerusalem: Bialik Institute, 1954.

Biblical References

Index

Also by J.W. Rogerson

The Poet Prophets of the Old Testament
Beauchief Abbey Lectures 2017 (2018)

The Case for Ernst Lohmeyer (2017)

Upside-Down Kingdom
Beauchief Abbey Sermons 2012-2015 (2015)

Cultural Landscapes and the Bible:
Collected Essays (2015)

The Kingdom of God:
Five Lectures (2015)

Perspectives on the Passion (2014)

The Holy Spirit in Biblical and
Pastoral Perspective (2013)

On Being a Broad Church:
An Exploration (2013)

Published by Beauchief Abbey Press
and available from www.lulu.com